LANGUAGES

in

INTERNATIONAL

BUSINESS

a practical guide

LANGUAGES
in
INTERNATIONAL BUSINESS

a practical guide

edited by

DOUG EMBLETON & STEPHEN HAGEN

Foreword by HRH The Prince of Wales

Hodder & Stoughton

LONDON SYDNEY AUCKLAND

British Library Cataloguing in Publication Data
Embleton, Doug
    Languages in international business: A practical
    guide.
    I. Title   II. Hagen, Stephen
    407
    ISBN 0 340 56790 2

First published in 1992

Typeset by Wearset, Boldon, Tyne and Wear
Printed in Great Britain for the educational publishing division of
Hodder & Stoughton Ltd, Mill Road, Dunton Green, Sevenoaks,
Kent by Biddles Limited, Guildford and King's Lynn

ACKNOWLEDGEMENTS

We, the editors, would like to thank all of the contributors for working against the clock in producing their chapters with enthusiasm and unreserved commitment to the book and its message. Without their contributions the book could not have contained the wealth of expertise and experience from within business itself. We would like to express our gratitude to friends and colleagues from the worlds of languages and business who have supported us and have encouraged us to promote the vital issues raised in this book. Particular thanks also go to Tim Gregson-Williams, publisher at Hodder and Stoughton, for wanting to make the book happen and for his advice and editorial guidance which assisted us in creating the final product.

Doug Embleton would like to thank the many individual users of the language services of ICI Chemicals & Polymers Limited whose feedback and comments over many years have assisted in the development of the concept of an integrated language strategy; all of the members of the C & P Languages Unit team, past and present; Edie Robinson, who makes any language training programme a joyful event; Andrea Cattermole, who so often proves that good PAs are invaluable; and, finally, Angela Embleton, Jennie and Helen for their patience and support during the preparation of this book.

Stephen Hagen would like to thank Richard Collinge and Alan Fletcher for their insights and observations which were quoted from the Manchester LX Centre's seminar *Talking to Europe*, organised by Mike Crompton, and which appear in chapter 3. A debt of gratitude is also due to Mr Joseph lo Bianco, Director of the National Languages and Literacy Institute of Australia (NLLIA), who provided data from the Australian Department of Foreign Affairs and Trade, on which the table on adult language learning rates on page 68 is based. Finally, a special thanks to Roulla Hagen for her unceasing support during the work on the manuscript.

NOTES ON CONTRIBUTORS

Graham Davies is Director of the Language Centre at the Polytechnic of West London. He has been working on computer-assisted language learning (CALL) for 14 years and has published widely on the subject. He has travelled extensively, lecturing and working as a consultant on CALL in 15 different countries. He is also a partner in a business specialising in the development and publication of software for students and teachers of languages.

Terry Doyle is Senior Producer, Languages, in the BBC Television's Continuing Education and Training Department. He has produced and directed many major BBC language series at all levels, as well as producing programmes about language teaching in the classroom. Most recently, he made the programme *Lingo! How to Learn a Language*, and is co-author of the book of the same title. He is also co-author of *Accelerated Italian* and is currently preparing a documentary series and video/audio pack entitled *Spanish Means Business*.

Doug Embleton is the Languages Unit Manager of ICI Chemicals and Polymers Ltd and has extensive experience both of providing, managing and developing language training, translating, foreign language publicity and language audit services for business. He is a Fellow of the Institute of Linguists and a Fellow of the Institute of Translation and Interpreting and is well known for his many active contributions in bringing together the worlds of business, languages and all levels of education. Co-author of the *Working with German* series, he has also developed the concept of an 'integrated language strategy' for business.

Heidi Gannon has a degree in German and joined Lloyd's of London's PR Department in 1986. She transferred to the Training Centre in 1988 and set up the language training programme which commenced in 1990. She now manages the programme and also provides some of the German tuition.

Diego Garcia Lucas is the Principal of Lancashire College. The college has developed into a centre of excellence in the sphere of language teaching, the production of open and distance learning packages, undertaking research into the teaching and learning of languages, and management training courses in the area of human resource development. Over the years, he has been closely involved in several European initiatives, most recently the coordination of a European project aimed at developing autonomous learning for weak learners in vocational education.

Stephen Hagen is currently Curriculum Director for Languages at the CTC Trust Ltd, London, where his work is sponsored by government in partnership with British business. He was responsible for managing the nationwide survey of Britain's foreign language needs, *Languages in British Business: An Analysis of Current Needs*, in 1988. Previously, he was Head of Newcastle Polytechnic's International Study Centre, responsible for international strategy, marketing and recruitment, as well as advising on language training for local business. At present, he is managing Europe-wide projects to develop industry-related language curricula and training materials for schools, colleges and business.

Helen Hancy is a graduate in German and Russian and has experience of teaching overseas and of specialist translation. She joined Norwich Union as European Research Assistant, initiated language training programmes and has been Language Unit Coordinator since 1990.

Geoffrey Kingscott is Managing Director of the technical translation company, Praetorius Ltd, which has offices in Nottingham, Leeds and Mulhouse (France). He is also General Editor of *Language International*, a journal for the language professions with a worldwide circulation, and is well known for his many other contributions to the enhancement of the translating profession.

Sir Peter Parker, LVO is Chairman of numerous companies, including Evered Barton Group, Mitsubishi Electric (UK) Ltd and Rockware Group plc. He is also Chairman of the Court of Governors of the London School of Economics. He has always encouraged the wider use of foreign languages by British companies and produced the UGC Report, *Speaking for the Future*, on the importance of African and Asian languages to British commerce and diplomacy. He was Chairman of The Japan Festival 1991. On 3 November 1991 he was conferred with the honour of the Grand Cordon of the Order of the Sacred Treasure by the Japanese government.

Bill Reed is a Director of Canning International Management Development. He now divides his time between developing and running business culture training programmes for British clients (he specialises in East Asia) and Canning's Italian subsidiary, of which he is the Director/General Manager.

Keith Robinson is a partner of Keith Robinson & Co., Chartered Accountants, based in Middlesbrough and is a graduate in Russian and French. His firm provides accounting, auditing and tax services to small- and medium-sized enterprises and is particularly interested in developing services for UK subsidiaries of companies in Western and Eastern Europe.

Anne Stevens is the Deputy Director of the Centre for Modern Languages at the Open University. Her experience is mainly in the field of language teaching and learning in vocationally oriented programmes and in employment. She has had wide experience of carrying out language audits and of designing and implementing training programmes. She is a member of the Standards Group of the Languages Lead Body.

Derek Utley is a partner of York Associates, a consultancy offering language services in a variety of languages to international companies throughout Europe. As well as being an active trainer in English communication skills, he is also responsible for languages other than English and for client contacts in Scandinavia and other countries. He is the author and co-author of several books and teaching materials in Spanish, French and German.

CONTENTS

KENSINGTON PALACE

In May 1990 I was foolhardy enough to accept an invitation
from Sir Peter Parker, the CBI and the Centre for
Information on Language Teaching and Research, to speak at
the Royal Society for the Arts on the challenge to British
industry and commerce of urgently making up for lost ground
in the learning of foreign languages.

In the two years since then the pace of international
change has accelerated even faster. New markets have opened
up virtually overnight with the final collapse of the
political and economic order in Eastern Europe and the
fragmentation of the old Soviet Union. In the European
Community the internal market of over 320 million people is
finally about to be born. Further afield, there are
positive signs of British companies gaining greater access
into the lucrative internal markets of East and South East
Asia.

Our pattern of trade continues to move steadily from
English-speaking countries towards Europe and markets
beyond. Trade knows no national boundaries and - although
English is the lingua franca of international trade - the
business environment is increasingly multi-lingual.
Britain's future prosperity and influence depend on improved
mastery of the languages of our trading partners.

Companies which wish to succeed in the new international
markets will increasingly have to adopt strategies which
take account of the cultural and linguistic barriers that
confront them. Written by a team of professional and
business people from small and large companies, this book
focuses on each of the steps that are necessary to develop
an integrated strategy.

Those at the sharp end of business who want relevant,
down-to-earth advice on how to 'make it happen' will find
this book both timely and appropriate.

HRH The Prince of Wales

PREFACE

SIR PETER PARKER, LVO

This is a time of unprecedented opportunity for British business. The business environment is changing as rapidly as the political map throughout Europe. The death of old political dogmas in Eastern Europe and the completion of the internal market in Europe have opened up vast new markets for our goods and services – virtually on our doorstep. The advent of the Channel Tunnel has effectively removed the last physical obstacle and given us access to an unbroken road and rail distribution network throughout Europe. The question now is how well British companies can overcome the remaining cultural and linguistic barriers that stand between them and the greater market opportunities that exist not only throughout Europe, but also worldwide.

In a changing context, two consistent realities have a bearing on why this is an issue for business in this country. We have become more dependent than ever on international trade: British exports have reached some 33% of GDP compared with 20% 20 years ago. It is also plain that trade is increasingly global in character and companies have to be international in outlook if they wish to compete and grow. There will be few sizeable British companies that survive into the next century without developing foreign partnerships, joint ventures or subsidiaries abroad.

But it is not only a question of trade flows and alliances, but also of how business operates. The trend towards an increasingly complex legal framework in which to do business in different countries of the world, the imperative to set up joint ventures and the indigenisation of management have major human resource implications for any company wishing to succeed in the ever-changing and fiercely competitive world markets – particularly in East and South-east Asia.

In brief, every company that wants to remain competitive has to develop a human resource development strategy which is responsive to today's world trends in an increasingly global market place:

- the growing pressures to enter joint venture agreements with non-English speaking companies;
- increasing tendencies towards linguistic nationalism;
- the pace of international communications demanding increasing international consultations;
- the acquisition of companies abroad and the increasing need to manage foreign workforces;
- the need to defend 'intellectual property' (patents, trade marks, commercial secrets, copyrights), especially in newly industrialised countries;
- the increasing need to travel to the traditionally non-English speaking parts of the world;
- the hiring and evaluation of agents abroad;
- the need to carry out market research and monitor techno-commercial intelligence via published literature from abroad;
- the increasing need to monitor international product standards, regulations and legislation;
- the increasing demand for transnational teams of managers;
- the imperative to conduct feasibility studies abroad for international projects; and
- the increasing demand for casual communication with foreign colleagues without the intrusion of local interpreters.

It is often argued that the growth of English as an international language means that British business people (as well as Americans and Australians) have a built-in advantage in the international marketplace without needing to study foreign languages or cultures. There is truth in this. The argument for an increased emphasis on foreign language skills is not intended to undermine the case for capitalising on this bonus from history. However, a belief in the 'English-only' approach can still be a disadvantage because it can encourage complacency, on the one hand, but, on the other, a lack of sensitivity towards the many *varieties* of English in business use and the hidden communication traps that await the unsuspecting '*English–English*' speaker.

Reliance on English alone will not be enough in many regions of the world – and the new markets are in overwhelmingly non-English-speaking countries. Fewer than 20% of consumers in the European Community have English as their mother tongue. If we add to this the peoples of Central Europe and Russia, the percentage of native English speakers across these markets becomes very small indeed. Finding a way into these new trading opportunities means knowing how to communicate in markets distinguished by diverse linguistic and cultural tradition, particularly in the countries of Eastern Europe. Linguistic nationalism is already a factor in certain areas of the world, e.g. Iran, Libya and some countries in Africa. In other countries like France, where the level of competence in English is higher, there is still, understandably, a marked preference for foreigners to speak French. This expectation, indeed, rises with growing economic dependence and a greater sense of national confidence – as in the cases of Korea and Japan in East Asia and now increasingly in Germany.

For example, Japan is the world's second largest economy and has a fast developing political role. The speed of Japan's technological advance and her capacity for innovative application underline the importance for any industrialised country of maintaining the closest possible links with Japan. A knowledge of Japanese language and culture can be invaluable to any British business wishing to enter this potentially vast market for western goods. It takes time and commitment to understand how to do business in Japan, and time is not available to most companies in the real world.

Moreover, without some understanding of local customs, it is easy for westerners to make mistakes, with potentially serious commercial consequences. Cultural awareness programmes are valuable, but cannot be taken far before some acquaintance is required with the language. The Japan Festival in 1991, I hope, contributed to a greater sense of understanding of how commercial trust can be built upon knowledge and respect for each other's culture.

Other non-English speaking markets are of increasing importance: China will have growing weight as the country with the single largest population of potential consumers. To operate successfully in China some knowledge of Chinese language and history is indispensable. In my experience, the chances of success in both these outwardly tough markets are significantly increased if business representatives are able to appreciate and work within the subtleties of the local environment. Language and culture awareness are an all-important means to this end – and are needed as much in Continental Europe as East Asia.

Given the intensity of competition that now exists for all foreign markets, every advantage must be exploited. Knowledge of local language and culture comes into play at many points and levels – and if you, or your organisation, are unable to operate an effective, integrated strategy abroad, you can be sure your competition has analysed and developed the capability necessary to operate locally and incorporated this within its own strategy. New markets have to be earned through a complex range of actions; for example, feasibility studies, collecting techno-commercial intelligence, communication with business associates, advertising and negotiation of complex deals. The markets – once won – are underpinned by ongoing and long-term responsiveness to customer requirements, including after-sales service and the manner of handling complaints. All of these functions require different levels of skills which companies need to employ in pursuit of their business objectives. Above all, in international business there is a need for a long-term strategy for overcoming the language barriers which can otherwise undermine the skills and confidence of the most valuable resource a company has – its people.

Language and culture run closely together. In my experience, training in both is essential if companies are to maintain a competitive edge in international markets and compete with local companies in their own domestic market. Second-hand knowledge from interpreters can soon be second-class knowledge; competence in a foreign market depends on talking to people in their own language, even if only haltingly from time to time, interpreting local information at first hand – even scanning local newspapers to get a 'feel' of local market conditions. I believe that the sharper our gift of tongues the sharper our competitive edge.

I am beginning to see that this view is also increasingly shared around the world. After all, what serious international company can afford to select its future leaders from people who are not as much at ease in Paris, Frankfurt, Rome or London, not to mention Tokyo? By the same token, any of a company's personnel operating internationally should have received the training to ensure that they are at ease.

When companies require expert advice, it is usually at short notice. When they want training for their staff, they are looking for intensive, flexible courses of a non-academic nature. An increasing number of leading companies throughout the world have already set up international human resource development strategies which put the stress on equipping their personnel to work alongside people of other cultures whether at home or abroad.

Major industrial groups like ICI Chemicals & Polymers, Thomson, Bayer, Siemens, Peugeot Talbot and, more recently, companies in the service sector like Norwich Union and Lloyd's of London have developed in-house language units which prepare people to handle business stretching across several continents. In some cases, the level of the investment is substantial – particularly by Continental companies. Siemens, for example, spends some £1.3 million per annum on language and culture training for personnel at all levels of the company – from apprentices to top managers – 40% on languages other than English. Even a medium-sized company on the continent like the champagne producer Möet et Chandon has set up its own language centre with plans to train the entire workforce of 2500! British in-company language units, however, do not always possess the financial backing or commitment from their senior management necessary to manage the same level of service as their European counterparts.

Our Community partners in other parts of Europe have also developed various strategies at the national level. Housed within the French Chambers of Commerce is a network of 150 *Centres d'étude des langues*. Each year some 60,000 people – mainly employees from small/medium-sized businesses – register for courses in a range of 22 different languages. Governments consistently play more than a passive role in this process; in both

France and Germany there are generous tax concessions to encourage companies to undertake language training, which do not exist in this country.

At the corporate level, our major competitors abroad benefit from longer-term thinking which produces a more consistent attitude towards investing in training at board level than tends to be the case in the UK. This is one approach which, I hope, will become increasingly adopted here as European economic union progresses. There are already encouraging signs. Recent reports show that most large British companies have actively reviewed their human resource policies in time for the completion of the internal market and that language training is the most common initiative being considered. However, training alone may not always be the right answer – which is why this book proposes a more strategic approach to all aspects of languages in business.

Simply put, your company may have the language expertise it requires already on the premises – yet without knowing. One area, for example, which companies should review in this respect is personnel policy. At present very few British companies currently have a clear policy on recruitment of staff with languages, the recording of existing language skills or the training of language or area specialists. Companies tend to recruit managerial staff for their personal qualities, and linguistic skill is in many cases of little account. In any case, the chances of matching technical competence, or product knowledge, to fluency in the foreign language is small. For example, there have been cases of companies overlooking the most obvious candidates for selection or re-training for jobs abroad, such as staff who already speak the language, if the personnel file includes no section on language skills.

On the surface, buying in expertise from outside the company on a temporary basis, rather than setting up an expensive ongoing training programme, can be highly attractive – but there are hidden dangers. Some companies feel that total commercial confidentiality would be better safeguarded by using their own trained personnel rather than take the risk of inviting in unknown 'experts', such as, for example, interpreters, who may not possess adequate technical or product knowledge or enough

understanding of the company culture for the job. Hiring nationals is another solution – but they will need quickly to develop a
feel for the company culture and have an adequate comprehension of English for the job they have to do. The greatest danger is,
however, if companies, or individuals, come to view the language
component in a transaction as a separate, free-standing component that can be 'bolted on' through a 'quick-fix' training solution.
The mistake here is to confuse the strategic and the operational in
the search for a simple, quick 'buyable' solution.

It is largely in response to the dangers of 'quick-fix' solutions to
complex language problems that this book has come about. Many
companies have now recognised that they can no longer afford to
ignore the linguistic and cultural demands of a market where they
have to think local and act global if they are to retain a competitive
edge. This book will at least provide them with the expert,
down-to-earth advice and practical solutions needed for the
development of an effective, long-term, human resource development strategy which incorporates languages.

CHAPTER ONE

LANGUAGES IN INTERNATIONAL BUSINESS

An Integrated Strategy

DOUG EMBLETON

MD'S DELIGHT OR ACCOUNTANT'S NIGHTMARE?

• Is such a strategy achievable? • What does it include? • Should it be given priority • It all sounds very expensive to me!

DEFINING THE NEEDS

• How are these needs defined? • Who should define them?

TRANSLATING AND INTERPRETING

• ... are separate activities and professions • Obtaining good translations • Using and interpreter • How much will all this cost?

PROMOTIONAL AND TECHNICAL LITERATURE IN FOREIGN LANGUAGES

• What is it? • How can I guarantee quality?

LANGUAGE TRAINING

• Setting the scene • Language training *is* management training • What the individual can do • What the organisation can do • Measuring progress

BUSINESS CULTURE TRAINING

- What is it? • How can it help?

The year: 2000. Carruthers & Co., a large international enterprise with a UK headquarters and parent company, has successfully extended its operations and organisation in Continental Europe and is now planning strategic moves in other parts of the world. Its integrated language strategy was initiated in 1993 and, since 1995, has been viewed as a key component in its own right. The strategy has played a significant role in supporting the company's transition to a truly international organisation.

Multilingual documents are translated and utilised to the benefit of the organisation and its customers; incoming enquiries, written or verbal, are handled efficiently; sales and technical literature is warmly received by local markets because it is written, produced and translated with these local markets in mind; language training programmes have yielded a tremendous long term benefit and staff identify with them and with the company's support for them; key members of staff exhibit a high level of cultural awareness in their dealings with foreign markets; overseas postings are well planned and supported. The atmosphere has become discernibly international and the people involved are stimulated by extremely positive personal benefits. The company and its customers, in turn, are experiencing a tremendous payback.

MD'S DELIGHT OR ACCOUNTANT'S NIGHTMARE?

Is such a strategy achievable?

Is the description of Carruthers & Co. simply a dream scenario or can it actually be achieved? Most organisations may not even have reached the dream stage yet and the issues surrounding language services and language skills remain shrouded in their own mystical aura. This situation has not been helped by the long-held assumption that modern languages are an academic subject and are somehow *separate* from the worlds of industry and commerce. It has tended to place industry or commerce on the one hand and linguists on the other hand on different sides of the fence.

Serious attempts are now being made to alert the world of business to the perils of ignoring the foreign language dimensions of the Single Market. During the latter half of the 1980s, '1992' emerged as a dream ticket for the burgeoning language services industry and a mass of organisations in the private and public sectors continued to extol the virtues of language services by using 1992 as some sort of 'sell by' date. Higher and further education colleges joined the ranks of providers, and government initiatives offered even more solutions. But did this leave the world of business any more enlightened in terms of what it should be doing? In many cases, it did not. Most of the 'languages and 1992' messages offered a blanket approach of 'languages are good for you'. So is cod liver oil. Up to now, there has been no serious attempt to match the issue of 'languages' with the ultra-practical nature of the world of business other than by these exhortation approaches.

One of the major arts of good consultancy is to leave the client with solutions and options which are indeed achievable and which relate specifically to that client's organisation. The aim of this chapter and of this book is to provide practical insights into the key components of an integrated language strategy. A foreign language strategy is undoubtedly of benefit to any organisation with international operations or opportunities. However, it is important to define the correct formulation and dosage. Above all, the outcomes of the strategy must be seen to be of sound practical benefit to the organisation's business activities.

There are no '10 Commandment' solutions and the success of any strategy will largely depend upon how successfully it has been adapted to the particular needs of the organisation. In setting out the practical parameters of an integrated language strategy the further aim of this chapter is to remove the shroud of mystery and build a bridge between the two parties involved. In order to eliminate the foreign language barriers to international trade we must firstly eliminate some residual barriers or misperceptions between the users and the providers of language services. If we do not do this, languages will forever remain a 'bolt-on' option locked in its ivory tower rather than an integrated component of effective international business.

What does the strategy include?

First of all let me demystify the term 'integrated language strategy'. It simply implies that those language services and activities which provide a vital support to the well-being and overall effectiveness of the organisation are structured and function in an interactive way. Unlike the knee-jerk reactions which are potentially engendered by the use of 1992 as a 'sell by date' the integrated strategy *is* allowed to gather its own momentum and to assume a degree of permanence within the organisation. The components of a language strategy are outlined in this chapter and are described in detail in other chapters in this book:

- language audits – the ongoing definition of language needs
- translations and interpreting
- sales and technical literature in foreign languages
- language training and business culture training

A Japanese friend of mine often used to reinforce his limited English with diagrams and drawings. It is amazing how one can convey a message of ultimate depth on a beer mat or table napkin! We were once discussing *integrated strategies* in a general sense and also with reference to the language issue.

He saw some organisations in this way (the titles are merely by way of example):

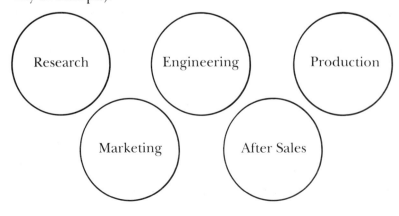

... and he saw *integration* in this way:

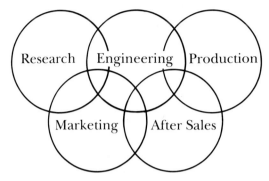

When I added my own artwork to the beer mat I positioned language services in what I termed the *interface* or *overlap* areas:

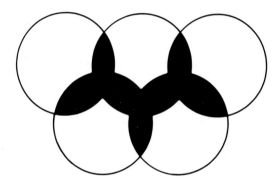

An *integrated language strategy* has to penetrate these interfaces. That is to say, it should be an ingrained aspect of the culture of the whole organisation that language issues are handled professionally and effectively since, along with all of the other functions and operations of the organisation, they contribute to overall efficiency. In this way, 'languages' can be viewed as a *single issue* rather than as a series of 'quick-fix' or 'first-aid' measures.

Indeed, as soon as any organisation becomes international in its activities (and this begins with the very first overseas contact or activity), the need for language services will emerge. A quick-fix, first-aid or bolt-on approach to these issues is inappropriate because:

- if the international nature of the organisation grows then so will its language requirements;
- if an organisation ventures into any activity with an inter-

national dimension – even that first dipping of the toe in the water – it surely wishes to succeed; if so, then one of the key issues of its internationalisation must surely be the language issue;

- if the language issue is not appropriately addressed the organisation will possibly *never* know how much 'not getting it right' has cost;
- the easiest alternative to a quick-fix is to do nothing (one wonders how many business issues involving a foreign language have ultimately received this treatment);
- any strategy is a *platform for improvement*: as overseas markets and contacts grow, the language strategy can be modified, extended or improved; without a strategy there is quite simply no basis for measurement; quick-fix approaches and their like can never be improved because they provide no platform; and
- staff involved with quick-fix approaches in any area soon become switched off and demotivated. Typical feelings engendered by quick-fix attitudes to language requirements are embarrassment and inadequacy. This reinforces people's views about their own island mentality.

None of this sounds too healthy for any organisation with international activities, does it? As the principles of 'Quality' tell us, there is a cost for getting it right and a cost for getting it wrong.

Quick-fix, first-aid or bolt-on approaches, if they persist, can also be an indication of one or several of the following:

- the tasks engendered (in this case by international business and by language requirements) are regarded as *irritants* or as being somehow *imposed*;
- nobody of influence within the organisation is willing or able to take a long-term view of the issues;
- the issues are not being addressed in a integrated way *simply because nobody in the organisation feels themselves to be on firm enough ground*; and/or
- the organisation has not allocated any *time* to the issues.

The diagrams earlier in this chapter refer to functions within a fairly large organisation in which, for example:

The Marketing function may have translation requirements (for contracts, correspondence and for promotional and publicity literature in foreign languages) and will surely have language training and business culture training requirements.

The After Sales Service function may need to handle overseas customer queries and complaints face to face (language training and business culture training) or by telex, fax or correspondence (translations). In turn, they will need to accurately convey customer requirements to the Marketing, Production or Research functions. This needs to be achieved accurately and promptly since most overseas customers have local suppliers *within their own country* who speak their language and are in a position to respond promptly. If your organisation has done the hard bit and has won overseas customers it surely does not make sense to allow any language barriers or delays to inhibit or impede its relationships with these hard-won customers?

The Research function will certainly need to keep up to date with the world technical literature and patent literature in its fields (translations) but, as overseas markets develop, the sale of products or services becomes as much a 'technical' sell as a strictly 'commercial' sell. Your product development experts may well need to speak with overseas customers to understand their product development requirements (language training). These, in turn, will be shared with the Marketing, Production and Engineering functions.

The more the international markets grow, the more language-related activities can be added to the integration diagram. The language requirements within these overlaps can be extended simply by extending the number of functional circles. For example, you could also include:

The Personnel Department – secondments and overseas postings; the personnel ramifications of joint ventures and acquisitions; database of existing language skills amongst staff . . .

The Transport Department – multilingual documentation for overseas transport . . .

The PR Department – sales brochures and product literature in foreign languages; exhibition materials for overseas . . .

The Legal Department – accurate and quality-guaranteed translations of sensitive documents . . .

The Patents Department . . .
The Market Research Department . . .
The Accounts Department . . . and so on.

An *integrated language strategy* means that all of the people involved at separate stages in the life cycle of a product or service will require these *separate* strands of a language service and will be aware that:

- they *need* them (people have to perceive the requirement before using the service!);
- these needs must be met professionally and efficiently for the overall good of the organisation; and
- these needs *can* be met . . .

via the integrated strategy, whether this means an internal centre of expertise or simply an internal clearing house to call in the most appropriate external support. As we will see later in the book, the same principles can be applied to small/ and medium-sized businesses. It does not matter what the size of the organisation is.

This book is intended to advise the reader on strategies, on how to 'get started', on how to ensure quality and on what to do internally and what to buy in. The rather negative quick-fix scenario can certainly be improved in many ways and this book provides positive and practical directions towards an integrated language strategy.

A good example of the interactive nature of an *integrated* language service occurred when I was once approached by a customer with a request for the urgent translation of some documents which were to be issued to the staff of a newly acquired company in France. Following several enquiries and discussions the language service was, within just a few weeks, involved in further translations of sensitive documents, liaison interpreting in meetings, the provision of language training and cultural briefing to staff involved in the project and the rapid revision of foreign language versions of sales and technical literature. The total package of services would have been tremendously difficult and expensive to buy or coordinate as individual components and the provision of the package at such short notice did much to enhance efficiency in those early and vital months of the project. In many ways these benefits to the project were perceived, experienced and acknowledged. However, it is often difficult to derive an accurate figure in hard cash terms to substantiate the value of the language services provided. This is undoubtedly a major blockage in the dialogue between providers and users.

A *permanent* strategy or service implies that its presence is accepted, just as we accept the need for insurance, the Fire Brigade or medical services.

Should the strategy be given priority?

In relative terms, *yes it should*. There will always be competing priorities in any organisation and business may well have wearied of the tub which 1992 enabled many providers to thump. Nevertheless, if we think in terms of 'Total Quality Management' we can observe that the main driving force behind any Quality initiative is constituted by the needs of an organisation's external customers. That is, the people who buy its products or services.

This is an excellent rule of thumb when defining the language needs of any organisation, large or small. It is very easy to misperceive language services as an internal requirement of the organisation whereas when correctly applied, they contribute greatly to meeting the market needs of customers and to enhancing the efficiency and performance of the organisation.

The cost of the *input* (language training courses are a good example) is not always measured against the benefits of the *output* (well-trained, highly motivated, culturally aware company representatives operating much, much more effectively). This is understandable because the *input* is a quantitative, financial parameter whereas the *output* is very much a qualitative issue.

Let us take the classic example with which our friends Carruthers & Co. were confronted. 'The after-sales service department must acquire some foreign language skills.' This is a limited rationale. We imagine that we know why this is a requirement. We probably *do* know intuitively. However, it is important to take the statement to a logical conclusion. This could develop as:

- *Why?*
- 'Because they feel exposed when dealing with certain overseas customers.'

- *In what way?*
- 'Well, for example, the problem often has to be resolved at workshop or shopfloor level where nobody speaks much English.'

- *Yes, but apart from that, what impact does this have on our business?*
- 'If the local agent is not there our own staff have real communication problems. Come to think of it, even if the local agent is there he is more of a salesman than a technical troubleshooter.'

- *And how do our customers feel?*
- 'I guess they are pretty frustrated at times.'

- *And how does this reflect on our company's image and efficiency?*
- 'Now that I come to think of it – not very well at all.'

- *Can you be more specific?*
- 'Yes. We waste time. We do not project ourselves as an *international* organisation. We are therefore not as good as the European competition in this area. Our person feels bad and this shows. We are losing vital technical information about competitors and about the performance of our machines because our person is having to rely on other people's language skills. He is marginalised ... and, yes, isn't this a pity ... because we have spent so much on researching, developing and marketing our products.'

The end result could well be a decision to examine the *long-term* language requirements of this particular function. This would be positive and permanent. It would also be cheaper than a rapid quick-fix decision to lay on some training for a few people. Unfortunately, the latter response has tended to be more prevalent.

It all sounds very expensive to me!

It has never been easier to waste money on the solutions to your organisation's language problems. It is not merely a question of *caveat emptor* but also of defining exactly what sort of service you want to pay for, whether internally or from external providers. In addition, an integrated strategy or policy implies a long-term approach.

Choosing the right language policy for *you* is what it is all about. It need not necessarily be expensive if it is correlated with the huge potential benefits which it brings. A balance has to be struck between the MD's delight at the obvious success of the strategy of Carruthers & Co. and the accountant's financial nightmare of relating the costs of the language strategy to these benefits.

Again, the strategy must be viewed in the light of its impact on the organisation's external customers. Customers are forever. They are difficult to attract and easy to lose. By the same token, good staff are an organisation's most prized asset. However, if they feel that they as individuals or that the organisation which they represent is not handling language issues well – or at all – this shows. Indeed, I constantly meet people whose ability to perform to their true professional and personal competence in any situation involving a language barrier is so severely inhibited that the international role which they could perform, but for this linguistic impedance, is at best a severe marginalising factor ('the linguistic and cultural wallflower') and at worst a severe demotivating factor. The culmination of these adverse effects does no good whatsoever for the organisation's image or business.

Most organisations naturally understand the concepts of research and development, marketing, patenting, advertising, public relations. These and other activities constitute essential ingredients in the life cycle of a product or service. Indeed, the individuals involved as specialists in these and other areas would all justifiably and proudly stand up for their contribution to the overall well-being of the organisation.

I believe that this is how professional linguists and people within the organisation who have personal language skills would like to feel. Unfortunately, the benefits of professional language services and skills are experienced by *individuals* in most organisations. It is an interesting and highly pertinent fact that I have never come across any single individual who, having felt the real benefits of either a professional language service or of language skills within themselves, has not:

- come back for more of the service when appropriate; or
- if at a personal level, wanted to develop the skills even further.

The acid test for any organisation is to ask these individuals about these benefits to themselves and, naturally, to the organisation. In the case of Carruthers & Co., the MD has also been on the positive receiving end of this equation. This helps but it will not be the case in many organisations. If it is not the case, it is still a very revealing exercise to check the responses of individuals to these issues. Typical responses which I have come across in surveys are:

'I find that more information can be obtained from people if they can talk freely in their own language rather than having to concentrate on speaking mine.'

'Our company is regarded in the German-speaking market as a "foreigner". It is vitally important that when called in to discuss or solve a technical problem we can give as good if not better service than our German competitors. This includes speaking their language.'

'The encouragement from my German contacts because I am making the effort is tremendous. It's a great ice-breaker.'

'I have a German friend in Germany who works as an after-sales technician for a German company. His company is a very successful one. Following an intensive English course which he was sent on some years ago he now receives an annual three-week 'booster' course. I have listened to him in sheer amazement when I think of the traditional attitudes which prevail in my own country. But as he succinctly explains: 'If I arrive at a customer's on a dark, and rainy Saturday evening and one of our machines has failed, the very last thing I want to say is "Do you speak German!"'.'

'An English friend of mine once worked as the project engineer to a major construction project in Spain. He had been granted the standard one week of intensive tuition prior to his departure from the UK and so had to rely on the English language skills of his Spanish suppliers. Things did not go at all well. There were frequent misunderstandings, late deliveries, false starts. He decided to learn Spanish with a vengeance and undertook this in his own time. He finally reached a stage when he could conclude discussions by asking 'Can we now repeat that in Spanish?'. Things improved tremendously. He put the cost benefits of his language learning exercise at between £1 and £2 million. Accountants take note!'

Before moving onto the practical components of an integrated language strategy, let us examine what does *not* constitute such a strategy:

An integrated language strategy does not consist of

- providing language training to staff on a short-term or unmonitored basis;
- stocking all of the available shelf-space in the Training Centre with self-tuition packages;
- pressing the panic button only when a translation requirement becomes an emergency;
- buying in a range of language services with no means of quality control;
- putting total faith in solutions offered by providers with very little or no hands-on experience of the worlds of industry or commerce;
- perceiving the issue simply as a staff training issue;
- delegating the issue of 'foreign languages' too far down the line without any sustained commitment from the top; or
- regarding the language issue as a *problem* . . .

. . . because if you do have a language *problem* this implies that you also have *opportunities* or *challenges* in overseas markets.

The integrated language strategy addresses these opportunities and challenges.

One quote which came from a language survey which I conducted several years ago has been a constant source of inspiration to me:

'My abilities in spoken Japanese, limited though they initially were, produced two main reactions from my Japanese customers. Firstly, an amazed silence. Secondly . . . respect.'

That simple statement says an awful lot. We cannot put a price on the financial payback in this situation. But we *should*.

I shall now describe the practicalities of the main ingredients of the strategy:

- defining needs
- translating and interpreting
- promotional literature in foreign languages
- language training & cultural briefing

DEFINING THE NEEDS

The ideal way to move away from the quick-fix approach is to take a step back and define the needs. This definition of needs is an ongoing process and is best conducted in collaboration with an expert consultant. However, it also demands the total commitment of the organisation.

How are these needs defined?

Several terms are used to describe the process of defining the language needs of an organisation:

- the language needs analysis;
- the language audit;
- the linguistic audit

I shall use the term *language audit*. Basically, just as it takes two to tango, it takes two to conduct an effective language audit. Both parties need to be very clear about the terms of reference and scope of the audit. It should be based on a thorough understanding of the activities, departments, markets, aspirations and, above all, *commitment* of the organisation.

For example, before proceeding with any language audit, the following questions could be addressed internally:

- Why do we feel the need for a Language Audit?
- What is our present policy on language-related issues?
- Have we even got a policy?
- What *are* the issues, as *we* see them?
- Who (especially people of influence) in the organisation holds strong views, either for or against, in respect of language issues?
- What is our overview of the benefits of any improvement in our language policy?

These questions may sound rather simplistic but then the most searching questions often do. However, they avoid the not unusual scenario of responsibility for the audit being delegated to one person in the organisation who may have no authority to implement any of the ensuing proposals and who, in the worst case, may have no realistic overview of their organisation's key language requirements. That person may not even be committed to any long-term strategy – or even to the issue of 'languages'.

The key to a successful outcome is the detail and scope of the preparatory work. The scenario depicted above could well deny access to the real issues.

The real issues may well be spread right across the organisation. Remember the Beer Mat Principle! Look in the right places.

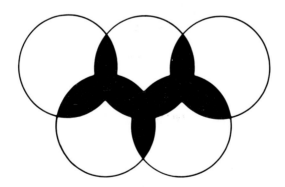

Remember that the key components of an integrated language strategy embrace documentation and training requirements and embrace, above all, the overlapping needs of various functions. Chapter 3 covers this in more detail.

Who should define the needs?

We have assumed that the organisation requesting the audit has already done its homework and has accepted that the results of any audit or consultancy will be a successful marriage of two views from two different angles. I hope that we *have* since, otherwise, we may as well simply go out and ask the language audit providers to conduct their own survey and tell us what to do. Unfortunately, most reports produced under these circumstances tend to gather dust.

In choosing a language audit provider it is important to find out what their mainstream activity is and what their track record of hands-on experience really is.

- Are they also selling their own language services as well as providing the audit? This is not necessarily a bad thing but you will obviously want to know.
- If they are, what is their specialism? For example, if the specialism is language training there could be a tendency to dwell upon language training as an over-predominant solution to your organisation's needs whereas in terms of those over-lapping circles above, training may be just one requirement or solution.
- At worst, the audit's recommendations could focus on certain services such as training simply because that is what the provider also sells. However, even if this is not the case, the provider's vision of what your strategy requires may well be impaired by their restricted experience of what solutions *are* available.
- What is their experience of the world of industry and commerce? Have they conducted audits for other organisations?

As with all areas of the language services industry there are good, average and poor providers. It simply pays to shop around, ask questions and get your own organisation's thoughts and commitment into some sort of order before plunging in.

The audit should address *all* of the areas relevant to your requirements. The 1990s will, I believe, see the emergence of the 'language consultant', one of whose mainstream services will be the language audit. Such consultants will also advise on good practice and will act as facilitators for individual projects. The use of an expert consultant for the languages issues involved in individual projects will be of particular benefit to organisations which have not yet fully implemented a language strategy. The organisation will already have acknowledged the need for a professional approach to language issues by its willingness to move towards a language strategy but, in the meantime, the language requirements of a key overseas project may have to be met immediately and at the same time as the project.

Before moving on to some brief and practical insights into the other main components of an integrated language strategy (translating and interpreting, promotional or technical literature in foreign languages, and language training and cultural briefing), one major issue needs to be clarified.

> Language training of staff is a key component in any integrated strategy but is *not* aimed at providing organisations with translators or interpreters or revisers of promotional literature, etc. It *is* aimed at creating high levels of communication skills which staff can use *appropriately, within their own specialist activities and within the limitations of their own, personal competence levels.* This distinction has to be very clearly understood within a language audit and within an integrated language strategy.

Other chapters in this book provide detailed and expert information on the possible individual components of a language strategy. In the remainder of this chapter I wish to prepare the ground for these detailed descriptions by very briefly highlighting some of the practical issues which you – the organisation or the individual within the organisation – need to bear in mind.

It is very important to make the clear distinction which I referred to above.

- Translating, interpreting and other specialist language services are provided by *full-time professionals* either within or external to the organisation.
- Language training and business culture training are also provided by *full-time professionals* but are an *enabling process* to enhance the *secondary* language skills of people whose *primary* skills reside in other areas of the organisation.

TRANSLATING AND INTERPRETING

As we will see in other chapters, translating and interpreting are complex, specialist skills. Clear distinctions have to be made between translations for the purposes of information and for publicity or prestige purposes. A distinction also has to be made between translating into English and translating into foreign languages. As with all specialist skills, the buyer generally gets what he or she pays for. However, it is important to link the translating costs to the total amount at stake in the project or situation which has led to the translation requirement. A good translation service will certainly provide 'added value'.

Translating and interpreting are separate activities and professions

These are two separate, specialist activities which people sometimes confuse.

- *Translation* is the conversion of written text in one language to written text in another.
- *Interpreting* is the conversion of verbal communication from one language to another.

As a general rule, professional translators concentrate upon translating and interpreters upon interpreting. These two activities are sometimes performed by one individual – for example, a staff translator who may be called upon to provide occasional interpreting as well.

Obtaining good translations

There are three main possibilities:

- establish an in-house translation service;
- send the work to a freelance translator; or
- send the work to a translation company or agency.

In-house

Several basic misunderstandings or misperceptions surround the issue of translation services. Of course, these apply only to a minority of users and these days competent translators are having much greater success in educating their clients. This may well be because whilst there will always be enough translation providers (staff translators, agencies, freelance translators) to meet market requirements, this is by no means an indication that they are all competent.

I believe that competent, top-quality translation providers – particularly in the light of the information and documentation explosion – will increasingly exercise the option of working for enlightened users. As described in other chapters on translating and interpreting, the best results are achieved when both provider and user share a desire for a quality end product and understand the means of achieving this.

What are the possible misperceptions?

- That staff translators cover *all languages* in *all subjects*.
- That translators require no background information on the subject in question.
- That translation is simply a re-typing process and that the concept of negotiated completion dates are a translator's eccentricity.

However, the benefits of an in-house translation service or even of one staff translator are varied. For example:

- The translator becomes familiar with your organisation and its particular needs and its specific terminology.
- Sensitive or confidential documents can be handled quickly and securely.
- The staff translator is the best person to buy in and quality control translations from external suppliers.
- An on-the-spot verbal readthrough or summary of a document can save you and your organisation a lot of time and money and enable you to take any resulting actions promptly.

That seemingly trivial and certainly brief telex or facsimile message may well reveal a potential order or a serious complaint from a customer. A 10-minute readthrough with the translator at your side may well involve a lot of money in terms of the issue involved.

In the midst of the information and documentation explosion, the in-house translation office can also become a clearing house and centre of expertise. Translations cost money and also need to be stored and indexed for future reference. A staff translator can also provide you with access to existing translations. For example, the rapid acquisition of that German Standard so vital to your project and required by tomorrow.

It is important to value your in-house translation service and ensure that it not only *feels* but actually *is* a real part of the organisation.

However, an in-house translation service is not always viable or cost-effective, especially for a small company.

Buying in translations (freelance translators, translation companies and agencies)

In terms of external suppliers of translations, just as is the case in many other service sectors, there are the good, the bad and the ugly!

- 'Large' does not always mean that the provider is reliable.
- You do not necessarily get what you pay for, but as a general rule the cheapest option is not only a risk but also a sign that you do not take your translation requirements seriously.

Translations are costed in terms of either the number of words (£x per 1000 words) or number of lines (£x per line).

Freelance translators specialise in specific language and subject area combinations. Be on your guard against the one person band who claims to cover almost every subject area and every language.

Highly competent freelance translators literally do it for a full-time living. They would normally belong to a professional body – e.g., the Institute of Translation & Interpreting – and have a clear background of experience. The 1992 bandwagon has seen the emergence of yet more small organisations claiming to be the answer to *all* of your language requirements. 'You name it, we do it.' Beware.

A truly professional freelance or a truly competent agency or translation company involves people who are highly skilled in the art of translation. They also want your repeat business.

Translation companies and agencies
Caveat emptor applies here as well. As a general guide you could:

- ask colleagues and contacts in other companies for recommendations;
- ensure that in the first stages of the relationship you have an independent element of quality control; and/or
- go and visit their offices if you can. A good provider will have no problem with this. On the other hand, you may discover that the glossy brochure and superb letterhead conceals a mere 'forwarding agency' operated by one person and a secretary.

Does all this sound a little too fraught? It is not really as bad as all that! There really are some highly competent providers. What can *you* do to ensure that things work at their best?

- Provide your suppliers with as much background information as possible.
- Provide them, in the early stages, with any relevant feedback or comments.
- Establish good lines of communication. A good external provider will welcome this. Beware those who do not.

And finally,

- Be receptive to any queries from your providers. It is a sign that *they too* want to get it right.

How should you use an interpreter?

It is not the purpose of this chapter to describe conference interpreting for a major event. However, you may need to use an interpreter within your own company or you may come face to face with an interpreting situation on a visit to another company.

I recall vividly the very first interpreting assignment of my career. I had been in the job for six weeks and was asked to interpret for some visiting French engineers. 'Is it a technical subject?' I timidly asked. 'Och, no,' replied the Scottish voice, 'all we're talking about is the arc-welding of some double-stage centrifugal air compressors.'

Rule 1
Do ensure that you give your interpreter as much background information as possible and do not simply regard a request for such information as a sign of any incompetence.

Rule 2
Interpreting methods can vary and must suit the occasion. However, do not get carried away by the stimulus of the meeting and convey two or three detailed paragraphs and expect your interpreter to do the same. Just try that exercise using English only with a colleague and you will see what I mean.

Rule 3
Interpreting can be very stressful and certainly demands a high degree of concentration. Remember that the interpreter is concentrating upon every word and every nuance whilst you switch off for 15 minutes in that important meeting. So ... give your interpreter, literally, a break!

Rule 4
Informal interpreting can at times be even more complicated than in the formal setting of a meeting. Conversations over dinner can drift from topic to topic. (At a later stage in my career I had three pre-rehearsed jokes in German and English. A short, a medium and a long one.)

Above all, remember that the more that *you* invest in helping the interpreter, the better the service will be.

How much will all this cost?

It is not the purpose of this book to specify any going rates. Indeed, rates for all language services vary just as the rates for consultancy, for example.

To return to the 'Accountant's nightmare' to which I referred earlier, the most reliable rule of thumb as to what you want to pay for translating and other language services is the importance which you attach to them *within the whole context of the job or project in hand*. If the job in hand only requires the linguistic equivalent of a Mini, then this will do. However, if the job is in the context of a valuable overseas market, a big contract or an essential piece of research, you probably need a Rolls Royce.

I think that as the translating profession develops it could – indeed, should – be prepared to charge per hour rather than on the basis of the number of words translated. A good example of this emerged in my own job during the writing of this chapter.

> We were asked to provide a translation into French of a draft contract involving a customer in a French-speaking country. The following activities were amongst the total number of activities involved before a quality end product was available:
>
> - ensuring that the French would be the type of French used in the target country (not France);
> - sourcing a competent external translation provider and negotiating a strict deadline;
> - revising the text in collaboration with the supplier;
> - inserting last-minute amendments and additions;
> - checking the subsequent comments and amendments received from the French-speaking party to the contract (three stages);
> - advising that some of these amendments were not simply of a linguistic nature but also had serious implications; and
> - seeking and incorporating expert linguistic/legal advice on these amendments.
>
> The end result was what the original requester wanted. However, there had been so much 'added value' from our expert services that any costing of the job simply on the basis of the number of words in the text would have been inappropriate.

'But we're spending all of this money on training the staff in languages, so why can't they carry out translations and be interpreters?'

The simple message is, in most cases, *forget it*.

Language training is essentially geared towards improving the communicative language skills of key personnel. These skills assist

them in the performance of *their* jobs within the organisation.
 Apart from anything else, such an approach:

- is unprofessional;
- takes people away from their primary roles; and
- consequently, can be more expensive than using 'the professionals' . . . and ultimately can be crushingly expensive in terms of the end result.

PROMOTIONAL AND TECHNICAL LITERATURE IN FOREIGN LANGUAGES

Here again, there is a Golden Rule. Professional translators translate *into their native tongue*. In general, all work of this nature should be prepared by people who are subject experts and who are working into their native language.

What is it?

What do we mean by promotional and technical literature? Well, it can be a glossy sales brochure, a technical manual, an exhibition display board, your product specification sheet ... anything printed in a foreign language for the benefit of your customers and aimed at supporting or promoting your organisation.

 I have for many years kept a collection of translation howlers which overseas companies have translated for the English-speaking market. They provide a humorous focal point of many a discussion or presentation.

 However, you need to imagine the situation in reverse if the documentation emanates from *your* organisation. These situations are a bit like being in a room and having an item of clothing undone. People don't always tell you! Similarly, you don't always get to know about poor – or even silly – promotional or technical texts until it is too late.

How can I guarantee quality?

- If you have an in-house translation office, allow them to coordinate the language component and organise quality control.
- If you use external providers and, assuming that you have already shopped around wisely, you should still have texts checked by somebody, preferably from your own organisation, in the *target country*.
- Ensure that texts are adapted to the market in question. For example, photos used in your own market may be inappropriate. Even colours are a sensitive issue.
- If you simply arrange for the translation of the original text it may well read like a translation whereas the objective is to persuade customers that you are capable of operating in *their* market in a way that at least matches the local competition.
- Decide whether a translation *or* a complete rewrite is required.
- Provide adequate checking measures *before* you do a final print. Otherwise, the changes can be very expensive.
- Above all, remember that the document or text in question may well represent the most influential and permanent reminder of your organisation. So, allow plenty of time and invest even more care and attention than you would in the preparation of an English text. Translation is a complex process, even when the end product is simply for information purposes. The preparation of high-class literature which will come into the hands of your *customers* – and your *competitors* – demands a high level of care and diligence. In my experience it is *never* simply a question of converting a text from English to another language. This topic is covered in further detail in chapter 12.

LANGUAGE TRAINING

Setting the scene

Well, here we are! We have finally reached the topic which most of the 1992 tub-thumping and mailshots were all about. I hope that I have been able to convince you that there are *other* strands to an integrated language strategy. However, language training is something which most of us have had previous experience of at school. Within that statement resides a whole separate chapter – or even a book – because it is true to say that for most of us the concept of language training, more than any other form of management training I know, sends us reaching for the clutch of pre-recorded clichés in our internal memory bank. 'Of course, I was never very good at languages at school.' 'We English aren't very good at languages, are we?' Yes, it often feels somehow like going back into the classroom whereas we feel more comfortable with that two-day quality improvement course or one-week computing course.

When one considers these programmed – and real – feelings which exist for many people, is it any wonder that many language training programmes have yielded limited success?

In tandem with this, the provider side of the equation has also had to adapt very quickly since some of the trainers involved have come from the teaching side of that very classroom. Indeed, some of the provider organisations have unavoidably *represented* that very classroom.

Language training is *management training!*

Now comes the good news! Trainers, publishers and language training organisations are beginning to recognise the specialist area which language training for business really is.

My own view is that language training for business is management training. It is separate from language teaching in schools, in Higher Education and in evening classes. It addresses realistic and real targets linked very closely to needs (the language audit). It succeeds when it is adopted as part of a long-term strategy either for you the individual or for your organisation.

It *has* to be gradual. However, it is no surprise that you the user can find yourself confused. Allied to the 1992 sales pitch have been the linguistically unsound claims from certain quarters of 'The one-week course' or 'Learn Swahili in four weeks or your money back'.

It is a pretty poor cocktail when you think about it! The pre-programmed self-evaluation of many individuals based on previous learning experiences coupled with the wild claims and sales pitches of certain providers. No wonder Fred, your Personnel & Training Manager, asks why you have not achieved fluency after two weeks of intensive tuition. No wonder your competent external providers grind their teeth when your first question is 'how long will it take?' (on the assumption that one or two weeks constitutes a long time).

So, let's define what *is* realistic and, above all, let's answer the key question . . .

What the individual can do

Subsequent chapters in this book examine in detail the wide range of language training options which are available to you.

However, in helping you – the individual or the organisation – to decide where to start it is useful to dispel one or two myths and allay one or two fairly common fears.

Will or should my language training be related to business or technology?

My own experience is that people need (and prefer) to study and master basic language skills before embarking upon 'business-specific' work. In fact, it is only when they have mastered the basic skills and structures that 'business' terminology is of any use. Until then, anything business-specific is simply a list of words and the language skills are rather like a car with no petrol. Once the car has petrol, then you can use some of your specific business terminology.

Will I make a fool of myself?

No! That is why I believe that language training for business *is* management training. The whole idea of any training for adults is to enable them to learn as adults with materials and an environment specifically designed for adults. Just as some of the concepts of vocational language training for schoolchildren are inappropriate because the world of work is not on their map of life experience, so the use of materials and classroom attitudes designed for young learners is inappropriate for adults.

But I've tried before and I didn't do very well

Well, perhaps you didn't have a strong enough reason or commitment? Or maybe you attended an evening class which contained too many students, of all ages and abilities, each with a different motivation.

Certainly, if you were a beginner, this would have switched you off immediately. Or possibly the teacher was not trained to teach adults? This can happen.

What the organisation can do

- Hopefully, the language audit in combination with your own organisation's perceptions and commitment will have identified some key language training requirements. The first thing which the organisation can do to ensure the success of any programme is to nominate a person as coordinator who is preferably well informed about or at least committed to language training. This makes sense if one considers not only the long-term amount of staff time and other expenses involved but also if one has signed on to the benefits which language skills will bring to your organisation. Not to do so is to deny commitment from the very start. To do so also makes dialogue with training providers so much easier and more effective.

- Make this commitment very clear to the staff who are to be trained. I have seen very few management training courses where non-attendance is tolerated. The same has not always applied to language training. Individuals have dropped out at will and organisations have not queried this.

- Draw up a Language Training Policy document which sets out, for example:
  — criteria for receiving language training;
  — the value which the organisation places on language training; and
  — the fact that it is supported *from the top*.

- Set up a Language Centre. At the start, this may be just one room. However, it will focus attention on language training. As it develops it could contain course materials, teaching equipment, magazines, videos, etc. Language training does not succeed half as well if it is viewed as nomadic in terms of searching for accommodation.

- Make clear distinctions between
  - *key requirements*: secondments and overseas postings, for example, require intensive tuition and business culture training which should be extended to other family members where appropriate;
  - *training for stock*: the long-term training of staff to cater for future requirements; and
  - *general interest*: there will be people who, if for holiday reasons alone, are interested in learning a language. Don't deter them. They can at least be offered some self-tuition materials and support.

Other chapters describe in detail face-to-face tuition, self-tuition, language learning materials, crash courses and business culture training. I will limit my contribution to two possible scenarios and some quotes from language training surveys which I have conducted.

Scenario 1. Your organisation has invested a lot of time, a major part of its management effort and a great deal of money and resources in a joint venture (. . . or acquisition, or overseas production facility, or market penetration in country x or . . .). You need to post three key members of staff overseas for at least two years.

In terms of their language training and cultural briefing your organisation may well be tempted to skimp in some way on the time allowed. This will either be because the individuals concerned are too valuable in their existing jobs prior to the secondment or simply because nobody in your organisation has a clear picture of what is involved.

In either case, bear in mind that the time invested in language training and cultural briefing will have a proportionate effect on the success of the two-year secondment. Think of all of the money and resources tied up in the project. In addition, think of the needs of the families of those individuals. They will also have to live overseas for two years and the happier and more settled they are the happier the secondment will be.

Scenario 2. Many years ago I experienced an interesting situation involving a person who had attended a two hours per week class in French for three or four years on a 'training for stock' basis. Suddenly, we had a very urgent and complicated technical problem in French-speaking Africa and he was the only technically qualified person involved with the product who could also handle the language issue.

Quotes from surveys have included:

'I travel to factory x where in general the lower management does not speak English.'

'I gave a lecture in German, reporting the results of a technical project. It was a terrifying experience at the time but the paybacks were tremendous.'

'I gained some very useful information from things I overheard during a visit by a trade delegation from x.'

'The mere fact that I am attempting to learn my customers' language has been received with tremendous warmth. The warmth has been like adjusting the radiator setting from 2 to the maximum 5.'

Measuring progress

This is a vital element in any language training programme. Two measures can be applied:

- regular assessments from the tutors or providers involved; and
- an agreed series of externally recognised, independent examinations. In my experience, I have found that learners are extremely enthusiastic about this approach, particularly when they pass the examination! It gives them a permanent sense of achievement and provides the organisation's records with evidence of the continued success of the training programme.

BUSINESS CULTURE TRAINING

What is it?

So, in some way or other you have developed an integrated language strategy which suits – and benefits – your organisation.

Business culture training is an important element in ensuring a smooth transition towards becoming a truly international organisation whether you are a large or small company – or even a one-person band.

Your strategy will have facilitated written and verbal communications with overseas markets. Business culture training enables you to improve your all round overseas capability even further.

Again, I will leave you to read the detailed description of what is involved in chapter 10.

How can it help?

Supposing you are dealing with French customers – or colleagues. Although you are well on the way to mastering the language you really don't know what makes them tick. Do you?

What makes them tick will be different from your own cultural background and upbringing. They will have different attitudes to business relationships, to negotiations . . . to life in general. This may emanate from their education, their upbringing, their values, their political system – the list is endless.

Some cultures prefer to keep business and socialising separate. In other countries, socialising comes before business.

Some cultures have totally different attitudes to formal meetings and discussions. In one culture it may be totally acceptable to brainstorm and alter the agenda. In others people may wish to stick rigidly to the agenda because they have prepared their contributions and nothing more.

Whilst business culture training does not dwell on any of these points excessively it provides you with an all-round awareness literally of *where the other person is coming from.*

In terms of overseas postings, cultural briefing provides an insight into life in the target country. It can help to smooth the integration of the individual into the overseas culture. Also, there will be instances when there quite simply is not time to learn the language in any depth whatsoever or where an individual is truly international in terms of the number of other countries visited. Suitable training can help to sensitise the use of English in certain situations so that you can feel sure that your message is understood. Have you ever talked with an overseas customer or colleague in English and wondered whether the smile *really* implied an understanding of what you said? You might be shocked to know the truth sometimes!

Post script

The year: 2000.

An integrated language policy was initiated by Carruthers & Co., in 1993. They went through the thought processes outlined here. They are now experiencing the benefits.

Dream scenario? This is no longer the case. There are practical ways of addressing these issues. Now that you know how and where to start you can begin to define your corporate or personal strategy. Give it a go! Your overseas markets are waiting for you.

CHAPTER TWO

THE LANGUAGE AUDIT

DEREK UTLEY

PREPARING FOR THE BALL
- Cinderella makes ready

SOME IMPORTANT QUESTIONS
- What is a language audit? • Why a language audit? • Who is it for? • Who can carry out an audit?

TOOLS FOR THE AUDIT
- Prerequisites: what the auditor and client need • Defined outcomes: what do you want from the exercise? • The role of the auditor: supplier too?

STAGES OF THE AUDIT
- Information gathering: the company • Information gathering: personnel • The questionnaire • On the day: the interview • Attitudes: notes for the auditor

THE DAY AFTER: THE REPORT
- Characteristics • Key sections • Implementation

MEMORANDUM
- Some underlying ideas

A FAIRY TALE ENDING?
- What will become of Cinders?

PREPARING FOR THE BALL

Cinderella makes ready

'Language audit' – the name says all: professional language competence, so long the Cinderella of Business UK Ltd, sheds her rags of irregular verbs and vocab lists, and dons her business finery for the corporate ball.

But will she meet the Prince and overcome all adversity, to live happily ever after?

It's all up to Cinders, really. The spectre of the Single Market proved to be her Fairy Godmother; and the DTI and the odd quango are at least as good as a pumpkin and a team of mice. So the scene is set for our heroine to go through her paces.

The aim of this chapter is to show what Cinders can do. Having put on her best frock, the rest of her life lies before her. The language audit is her entry to the ball; everything else depends on her performance: her wit, her experience, her flexibility.

So how can she prove her worth, and not only become a princess, but also bring peace, prosperity and happiness to the kingdom? Or, more prosaically and more importantly in this case, swell company profits? Yes, the bottom line is everything, but before reaching it, there remain . . .

SOME IMPORTANT QUESTIONS

What is a language audit?

It is an exercise in defining:

- any foreign language skills existing in a company;
- present and future needs for language skills, internal or external;
- the people likely to require them, to what extent and to what purpose;
- optional pathways for developing skills to bridge the gap between needs and present competence; and
- when and how to buy in outside services to cover short- and

long-term needs in documentation, translation and interpretation.

Why a language audit?

- Because any company involved in anything other than totally parochial business needs to consider whether the constant and sole use of English as a business medium is:
  — efficient;
  — satisfactory; and
  — polite.
- Because language skills are not easily available in the English-speaking world – blush, you captains of industry – nor are they easily or cheaply developed, or cheaply bought in.
- Because a thorough and professional approach to locating and developing these skills will be more efficient and cheaper than any 'quick fix'.

No company has its information systems chosen and installed by somebody trained on the basis of two hours a week at night classes. Nor should they entrust their foreign language communication to the same system.

Who is it for?

- For all large organisations.
- For organisations with international contacts of some sort.
- For organisations threatened by foreign competition.
- For organisations keen to grasp opportunities offered by the lowering of trade barriers and the opening up of new markets.

A decreasing number of firms will find themselves outside all these categories!

Who can carry out an audit?

Any foreign language consultancy with the characteristics and experience mentioned below (see page 36).

Foreign language consultants are a relatively new but growing breed. They also tend to be *suppliers* of professional language services – see 'The role of the auditor: supplier too?' below for a consideration of this possible dilemma.

TOOLS FOR AN AUDIT

Prerequisites: what the auditor and client need

Certain attitudes, skills and physical conditions need to be available on both sides.

The *client company* must start out with a commitment to the following:

- a coherent policy towards communication with non-native speakers of English, whether they be clients, colleagues, fellow professionals or suppliers: which languages are acceptable and when;
- a clear commitment to the acquisition or development of professional language skills and services;
- the inclusion of language skill development in the career plan mapped out for selected individuals by the personnel department; and
- the availability of resources to fund the above.

In addition, the client company needs to provide:

- time and resources for a complete briefing on the structure, operations and aims of the company, particularly in the international field; and
- space and time for interviews with employees.

The *auditor* must have:

- the professional, business approach of any consultant;
- real experience of a range of companies: how they are organised, how they act, what their objectives are, how people behave within them;
- fluency in at least one foreign language;
- experience of multilingual and multi-cultural contacts within a European or world business environment; and
- qualifications in, and experience of, the provision of profes-

sional language skills: training in language and cross-cultural contacts; translating and interpreting; original documentation.

It is worth stressing that if any of these conditions are missing to any degree, it will save a lot of time, effort and money in the short term not to bother; in the long term, however, infinitely more will be lost. Cinders may as well go back to peering into the ashes.

Defined outcomes: what do you want from the exercise?

One of the first things to be decided on both sides – auditor and company – is the outcome of the exercise. The obvious products will be:
— a clear written report; and
— an interview to discuss and clarify the contents.
What will be less obvious is what the report will present by way of recommendations either as a set of solutions or a range of options. The second choice seems preferable in most cases, as final solutions will depend to a large extent on resources of time and person power and on the company's own internal priorities.

The role of the auditor: supplier too?

The auditor will almost always be a potential supplier, and as such may be tempted to make recommendations that tie the company to her/his services. Personal trust and confidence come into play here; a simple yet seemingly harsh solution may be to make quite clear when choosing the auditor that s/he will not be a bidder for any services put out to tender as a result of the audit.

STAGES OF THE AUDIT

Information gathering: the company

Once it has been decided that an audit will take place under the conditions described above, the auditor will make contact with at least one senior member of the company in order to discuss and receive relevant documentation on:

- products and markets;
- organisation;
- types and number of personnel;
- present contacts with non-native speakers of English;
- plans for expansion, joint ventures, takeovers;
- incoming documentation in foreign languages, and outgoing correspondence and publicity material; and
- attitudes to recent takeovers, mergers or joint ventures.

Unless the auditor gets a feel for the company, as well as factual information, his analysis risks being incomplete or shallow.

> A small firm of makers of precision instruments for scientific research has discovered its products are extremely competitive in the German market. At present it supplies only clients in the South of England. It plans to set up contacts with agents, marketing firms or, preferably, clients, in order to establish a sales network in Germany. One administrative assistant has German 'O' level from eight years ago. An auditor is briefed on the firm's activities, personnel and immediate targets as recommended by a marketing consultant.

> A national manufacturer of packaging material is taken over by a French company. Middle and upper management receive lots of documentation in French, and attend meetings where French has to be interpreted, and halting English understood. About half of these managers have French 'O' level or equivalent, typically from 30 years ago. The auditor is told initially of the terms and early experience of the takeover (hostile or friendly?), the attitude of the new owners and the British company's managers, and of the likely impact of the takeover on the future of the British company and employees.

Information gathering: personnel

Equipped with this preliminary information, auditor and company representative will need to collect more detailed information from those employees most likely to be involved in language development. Usually, sales and marketing people are the first to come to mind, but although they will provide the first thrust for a company moving into export, a company with international connections will have a multiplicity of requirements.

Typically, these requirements will cover a wide range of language activities: training, cultural briefings, publicity material and interpretation for key contacts. A clear distinction needs to be made early on between what these activities are, and what they can achieve in their different ways.

Key personnel likely to be considered for language development:

- marketing and sales;
- research and development;
- information systems;
- telephonists/secretaries;
- after sales service; and
- public relations.

A certain category of personnel – Very Important People, real or self-styled – may have a very strong reaction to foreign languages: they may get over-excited and try to burst in on the act, or they may run a mile. In either case, they should be treated with discretion and concern.

The questionnaire

The most convenient way of collecting this written information is by means of a questionnaire, which will elicit the following:

- name and age range (e.g. 25–30, 40–45);
- job title and functions;
- present contact with foreign speakers;
- possible future contact;
- types of contact (read, write, talk);
- qualifications or history of language learning (languages, levels); and
- subsequent language experience.

> *Rules for questionnaire (and for most written communications in life!)*
> * Keep it short – never more than one side of A4.
> * Keep it simple – short phrases, short words, no jargon.
> * Give a brief reason why the questionnaire is being sent.

The questionnaire will form the basis for an interview with all those concerned, or of representative samples where large groups are involved.

On the day: the interview

Practicalities

If more than one language is likely to be used/assessed in the interview, and the auditor is not competent in all of them, s/he will need to take a colleague to make sure all languages are covered.

The number of interviews conducted will depend on the number of employees under consideration, and the resources available. Where there are groups with similar characteristics and likely needs, such as a group of young recruits or of office assistants, a representative sample may be taken.

A quiet room will be needed for the interview.

The company representative will have worked out a timetable for interviews, allowing some 30 minutes for each interviewee, plus necessary breaks. Physically and mentally, it should be possible (for the auditor!) to do 12 good interviews per day.

Attitudes: notes for the auditor

Most British people have various layers of emotional reaction to foreign languages (OK, to foreigners too), ranging from assumed insouciance to deep terror; so the atmosphere of the interview should be warm and relaxed, in order to peel off as many of these layers as possible. And to avoid possible heart attacks. An easy way of warming up is to check the contents of the questionnaire.

Another good settler is to establish with the interviewee a clear understanding of the auditor's role and the purpose of the interview.

What to talk about

As the auditor checks through the questionnaire, more details of the interviewee's job will emerge. Time should be spent on this, as explicit and implicit details uncovered here will have direct bearing on language needs.

If there is evidence of a basic competence (say, five years' language learning at school) the auditor should gently warn that a few words of target language will be used at some point during the interview to assess comprehension and possibly speech.

The main areas to be covered in the interview are:

- details of types of present and possible contacts in foreign language:
  - will they be by letter, phone, face-to-face, large meetings;
  - will they be formal, informal, social;
  - will they be friendly or potentially hostile;
  - will they involve specific work topics, general business, or general chat; and
  - will there be any difference in hierarchy between the participants.
- frequency of contacts;
- the degree of urgency and/or keenness shown by the interviewee;
- amount of time likely to be available for language development;
- any personality characteristics likely to affect membership of a learning group, i.e. group dynamics;
- any characteristics of learning style which might affect learning methods;
- level of competence in the language. For this the auditor will need to carry (in head or briefcase):
  - a range of topics/questions to be understood and/or answered; and
  - a scale of levels of language competence on which the interviewees can be placed, and which will make some sense to the company (see below, 'The report'); and
- in the case of potential users of translation and interpretation services:
  - volume of traffic;

— types of documentation produced/needing to be produced, with examples; and
— types of encounter.

No two interviews will follow the same order or pattern. The auditor should keep a clear checklist of all areas to be covered, but should concentrate on developing a natural, relaxed conversation following its own logic, rather than on conducting an interrogation.

Typical employee profile resulting from an interview

Company: British subsidiary of an electronics company recently taken over by a French multinational.

Employee: 45-year-old logistics manager responsible for material flow.

Contacts in French: ill-defined and at present slight, but with likelihood of increase. At the moment, meetings are with high-level managers who speak reasonable English, but increasingly contacts will be with people from information systems, distribution and production people, whose English will be limited or non-existent. Many contacts at the moment are informal and social, in France and in Britain.

Language competence: 'rusty O grade' 30 years ago; little contact since, but some interest in French shown by fairly regular holiday trips. Can understand basic questions about family, house, town; and reply hesitantly and inaccurately (rough transcript available).

Motivation: slightly apprehensive of job and language, but keen at the same time.

Learning characteristics: learnt by grammar grind, realises need to speak. Easy-going character.

THE DAY AFTER: THE REPORT

Characteristics

The findings will normally be carried in a formal report to the company, delivered within a few days of the interviews. Here, as in the questionnaire and elsewhere, the essential characteristics will be brevity and simplicity. The following topics should be covered:

- management summary;
- introduction/scope/background;
- objectives;
- procedure adopted:
  - the questionnaire;
  - the interviews.
- results:
  - typical profiles;
  - main needs identified (training/development and language services);
- options available; and
- appendices:
  - the questionnaire;
  - assessment scale used;
  - list of interviewees and levels.

Key sections

Of these sections, two warrant further study:

Options available

The framework for this section can be standard reference, compiled from the auditor's experience, and held on computer.

Although the same information will be found elsewhere in this book, it is worth outlining the main questions to be considered here.

Purchasing: buy translation and interpretation to solve immediate needs. Build up relationship with reliable supplier(s) whose quality standards are high, especially in speed, accuracy and appropriacy.

Recruitment: recruit linguists where possible – a long- or medium-term solution!

Personnel planning: posting or rotation of chosen staff in different non-English speaking countries, in order to acquire experience of language, cultural diversity and company practice. Also, individual development plans to include consideration of development of language skills and cultural awareness.

Personnel training: a number of decisions to be taken here! The auditor's detailed advice, depending on company needs, language profiles and levels will be specific and crucial. A checklist will include:

- intensive (blocks of one whole day or more) or extensive (so many hours per week)?
- self-access learning, or teacher-led, or a combination of both?
- group or individual?
- inside the company or at a local training centre?
- in the UK or abroad?
- fixed times or ad hoc?
- specified length of training period at beginning?
- specified level as objective on internal scale or external exam?
- continuation or maintenance training thereafter?
- assessment and reporting procedure?
- cultural awareness seminars?

Assessment scales

Few standard descriptions of language levels exist which are acceptable both to linguists and to managers. Any consultant worth his salt will have or produce one which is adapted to a particular client's needs and perceptions.

Implementation

Implementation rests with the commissioning company. Short-, medium- and long-term implementation of the options offered is the crux of the whole exercise. It is the area where Carruthers and Co., at time of press, are performing ingloriously.

The report, promptly delivered, will be the basis for discussion between auditor and company which will end in the formulation of an action plan.

MEMORANDUM

Some underlying ideas

As in most aspects of life and work, language audits consist of a lot of preparation and detailed hard slog.

But there are also some key facts, ideas and principles which should inform the whole exercise and at the same time motivate the players.

- The Brits are indisputably low on the foreign language competence chart. Given the increasing acceptance of English as a world language, our international colleagues have shown greater inclination and stamina in learning English than we their languages. This is tough luck for the Brits but, paradoxically, two outcomes of this situation should motivate us:
  — the predominance of English has prompted a mini backlash, in which native speakers of English who speak other tongues are not only prized for their rarity value, but are actually *insisted upon* by some foreign clients; and
  — the boom in the learning and teaching of English has produced a bank of expertise which only now is being fully exploited by teachers of other languages.
- Quality documentation is not only appreciated; it gets results.
- Developing language skills from a typically low level (in comparison with our European neighbours) can be a long, arduous and potentially expensive job, whatever methods are employed. Skimpy input at audit or later stages will give skimpy results, and waste money.
- On the other hand, a job well done will be good for the bottom line. And do a lot for staff morale. This has been proved in many cases.
- A language audit, and all language development work, requires total commitment from the company – as does any develop-

ment project. This implies time and money, the involvement of an authoritative company representative, and the adoption of a sense of partnership between company and language consultant.

• A language policy sits within an overall corporate communication policy, and also within a human resource development policy. In the former, all documentation will conform to total quality standards, and all meetings with non-English-speaking clients and colleagues will be guaranteed optimum understanding; in the latter, types of personnel will be identified as needing language skills, and as being eligible for specific kinds of training to acquire them. Language skills will figure on the agenda of appraisal interviews for a large percentage of people.

A FAIRY-TALE ENDING?

What will become of Cinders?

No precise details are available as to what happened to the Prince and Cinderella. 'Lived happily ever after' is OK, but begs many questions about the kingdom: what happened to the rate of inflation, for example, or the balance of payments, or the eternal nag of unemployment?

We may never know, but the signs certainly looked good when last we heard.

Perhaps in our case, too, Cinderella is moving beyond the stage where she has just the frock and the glass slippers. The coach awaits, the music swells in the background, the courtiers are gathering, the Prince is expected. Some of the courtiers look a bit shifty and suspicious, it's true.

But Cinders looks great, and there's a glint in her eye. Maybe it will all work out . . .

CHAPTER THREE

EFFECTIVE LANGUAGE TRAINING STRATEGIES

STEPHEN HAGEN

'Efficiency is doing things right; effectiveness, however, is doing the right things.'
(*Peter Drucker*)

DEFINING AN EFFECTIVE LANGUAGE TRAINING STRATEGY

• So where do you start? • What does it involve for your company?

THE STEP-BY-STEP APPROACH

BRAINSTORMING THE IDEA

• What are the issues? • Internal strategy – a checklist

REVIEWING THE NON-TRAINING SOLUTIONS

• What are the alternatives to training?

DRAWING UP A TRAINING SPECIFICATION

• Training goals and corporate priorities • The supplier's specification

CHOOSING THE TRAINING SUPPLIER
- What are the options? • Selecting a good supplier

IMPLEMENTING THE TRAINING SCHEME
- How long does it take to learn a foreign language? • Can you spot good learners? • Can you spot good tutors?

MEASURING AND EVALUATING OUTCOMES
- Ensuring value for money

FOLLOWING UP

DEFINING AN EFFECTIVE LANGUAGE TRAINING STRATEGY

'Disaster quickly followed our arrival in Madrid, where we soon found out that no-one we met spoke English . . . our samples are still probably somewhere in Spain. The potential customers given to us by the British Consulate either had moved or couldn't understand us when we did catch up with them. The exhibition was dominated by the Italians who appeared to speak Spanish or had interpreters – so we came home feeling very despondent and just a little foolish! I vowed then that I wouldn't make the same mistake again and have the arrogance to expect that everyone should speak English.' (Alan Fletcher, MD, Archer Security Products Ltd)

Many companies like Archer Security have experienced a similar baptism of fire in some foreign land before deciding on a strategy to cope with language problems. With the globalisation of trade and the increasing number of cross-border activities, the likelihood is that almost every company will need to consider what to do about languages sooner or later. The first thought is often to 'buy in' training for staff who seem to need them most, which is for those who *initiate* or win business on the export/sales side of the company. But then there are the less obvious cases of employees who *maintain* the business, who are either in daily contact with foreign clients or who occasionally meet the kind of communication problem at the first point of contact that can irretrievably damage the business – the receptionist, the gateman, the long-distance lorry driver, the secretaries and, of course, the MD, who also needs a few words of foreign eloquence for those grand moments abroad.

So where do you start?

Language training requires a strategy within an *integrated languages strategy* – simply because of the vast range of choices and their associated pitfalls. This chapter is intended to provide you with a plan to decision-model your way through the bewildering sets of options and make informed choices about the best course of action.

Chapter 1 will have given you an idea of your needs in depth, but you will still be faced with a bewildering array of language learning solutions. On the one hand, the shelves of shops bristle with the latest tutor-less DIY language kits which offer the promise of 'instant' success – sometimes in as little as three and a half weeks, occasionally even less. There is the allure of new technology, ranging from passive hand-held electronic translators (which claim to do away with the need to learn languages altogether) to self-tuition systems, such as interactive training videos, satellite broadcasts and computer programs.

Then, on the other hand, there is the traditional classroom approach, which – unlike the image many of us retain from our schooldays of learning irregular French verb tenses by rote – nowadays offers exciting new methods, new combinations of courses, a choice of native speaker or non-native speaker tutor and a variety of locations. You may have to choose between the local tech, for example, which tends to run group evening classes at unbelievably low prices, and the up-market somewhat glossier private language school, which will organise one-to-one 'crash courses' to suit your exact needs. The cost of learning a language can vary from a few pounds for a DIY book and a few cassettes to around £1000–2000 per person for a week of intensive residential tuition.

In fact, the solution for your company may be all of these

possibilities, none of them, or, more likely, a combination of the various options. There are so many variables that the best solution requires a strategy – which, as outlined in chapter 1, is an integral part of a broader corporate strategy for languages. Ideally, language training is an increasingly vital aspect of international human resource development and, as such, should be reviewed in the corporate plan and resourced as part of business training. The company stands to gain in two ways. There is an immediate pay-off: initial language problems will be solved – but, in the longer term, the training will help the company grow in world markets by encouraging employees to think globally, i.e. to view business from a worldwide, rather than from a local or national perspective, whilst, at the same time, fostering good employer/employee relations. After all, language training can be a popular and effective part of individual, as well as corporate, development.

What does it involve for your company?

Implementing a language training strategy is rather like building a house – once you have a rough sketch of how you envisage the final outcome, you call in expert advice – initially, your architect – to match the *desirable* to the *possible* in the light of such inhibiting factors as the timescale, the building's purpose, location and the available budget. The same process applies to setting up an effective language training strategy; it means introducing the same degree of professionalism into your planning as you would for any other major long-term investment or purchase which involves your most prized asset – people. In most cases, this means employing an independent consultant to assist you in the design and implementation of the *right* training strategy to suit your company's specific profile.

The 'building blocks' of a language training strategy would be: *the tuition* (e.g. face-to-face, self-tuition); *the mode* (e.g. crash course, regular weekly); *the choice of learning materials or media* (e.g. braodcast video); the use of computers; the *content*; and *business culture training*. Each of these choices is looked at in later chapters, but, first, you have to decide whether or not you need a language training strategy at all!

It is quite common for businesses in this country to buy in language training from the Yellow Pages when a sudden need arises. The kind of 'Quick! Call in a language trainer' approach can be effective in the short term – provided the company is lucky and happens to pick out a supplier who is both professional and competent. On the other hand, if the company is seeking more sustained international activity than a one-off contract or query, a more medium- to long-term training commitment is worth careful consideration. In other words, a company that intends to stay in the international market needs to think in terms of 'training for stock', rather than 'training in the after-shock'.

THE STEP-BY-STEP APPROACH

It is possible to design a language training strategy by working through a series of seven steps – as outlined below – and develop a customised plan of action for the company.

A seven-point strategy

- Brainstorm the idea.
- Review the non-training solutions.
- Draw up specifications.
- Choose a supplier.
- Implement training scheme.
- Measure and evaluate outcomes.
- Plan follow up.

BRAINSTORMING THE IDEA

The language audit discussed in chapter 2 will be a good starting point for brainstorming the various solutions, which may or may not include training. It is up to the company how it wants to address the issues raised by the audit. At this stage the recommendations have to be set in the context of your company's plans and business strategy – which requires applying the kind of knowledge and understanding of internal company politics which, often, only someone on the inside can do. The auditor can only recommend – the decisions have to be made by the company after that.

What are the issues?

The first stage in setting up the strategy is to brainstorm the options from within the company – so that any decision taken is fully owned on the inside. The kind of issues that will be raised relate to questions on the finance, commitment and results expected by the company:

- Why do you think foreign language training is the *only* solution?
- Have you estimated what the likely benefits are for the company?
- Which budget will be used for the training?
- Who will co-ordinate the training from within the company?
- Which managers should be consulted?
- Can the company afford the commitment?
- Is language training compatible with the company's culture?

Whether the company's structure and culture can accommodate a potentially expensive medium- to long-term training solution is a key issue. There may be insurmountable cultural barriers to the idea of language training in your company. An effective language training solution entails changes in attitude, lifestyle and culture by people at various levels in the company. Some managers and employees, for example, may feel that 'English is enough' and view language training as an expensive luxury with only limited value in the 'real world'. If senior managers (or the MD) hold the view that 'everyone speaks English anyway, so why bother?', you will need to bring the issue out into the open and clear the ground of any lingering prejudices. Otherwise, they will ultimately undermine the success of any training solution by demotivating the learners before they begin. When you come to present the case for financing language training, remember that the training is simply a mechanism for achieving *corporate* or *strategic* goals. This means that the more closely language and culture training are integrated into the corporate human resource development plan, the better understood it will be throughout the company. But if you find you can't alter attitudes, then you may have to think in terms of encouraging any potential language learners to do the training in their own time – and possibly just apply for a subsidy from the company.

For the training to succeed, everyone concerned should be aware that this is a solution which is based on a tangible business need. In this respect, the audit is very important. It will serve as the foundation for a language training strategy which meets corporate goals and addresses the gaps identified by individuals in their work. The internal discussion process can be summarised in a checklist.

Internal strategy – a checklist

Have you

- checked that adequate finance is available before considering the solutions;
- identified the decision-makers who would need to approve the training;
- gauged the reaction of the line managers towards the possible absence of key staff;
- identified a suitable location for the training;
- considered what physical obstacles there are to running an in-house language training programme (e.g. on-site accommodation); and
- pinpointed who will implement, oversee and evaluate the language training programme?

REVIEWING THE NON-TRAINING SOLUTIONS

At all stages you should also guard against the 'surgeons-always-recommend-surgery' syndrome, which may come out of the audit report. If the language auditor is a language trainer, he or she may tend to analyse each skills gap as a training need. You should check whether any needs identified at the various levels could be resolved by other courses of action, possibly involving other departments, such as human resources (or personnel).

What are the alternatives to training?

Try out these non-training solutions – they may be far less costly and time-consuming in the long run!

- Build up a database of employees with existing linguistic skills.
- Offer a system of incentives to employees who pass exams in the required languages.
- Re-locate staff with appropriate skills to the areas of deficiency.
- Hire foreign nationals.
- Include requirement for language skills in all your company's job adverts.
- Transfer a colleague from a foreign subsidiary or associate company abroad.
- Buy in consultants as and when needed to deal just with language tasks.
- Send personnel to a subsidiary abroad for language training.
- Acquire an operating company abroad, which will handle your language needs.

DRAWING UP A TRAINING SPECIFICATION

Whichever solution you choose, whether or not it is one of the recommendations offered by the language auditors, it has to be derived from what is feasible for your company. During the brainstorming process, you will begin to formulate aims and goals.

Training goals and corporate priorities

Your company's primary business aim will be *to achieve corporate goals by measurably improving job performance through identifying the specific language and culture training needs of individuals in the company and ensuring that the training programme meets them.* The short-term goals will be more specific – based on the immediate needs of the company. If you are responsible for overseeing the training, you should formulate what you require the training to achieve in two short specifications. The first is for your own company; it incorporates a rationale for the training and a brief business plan, which you should copy to key people in your company on a need-to-know basis (but especially the budget-holder!). It should contain statements on:

- the company's problem: in terms of individual language needs and corporate priorities;
- the training goals;
- the most appropriate options, extracted from the language audit (which you can append);
- any potential obstacles to implementation (e.g. corporate, departmental culture, staff availability);
- the proposed timescale – including training goals and monitoring procedures;
- the facilities which may be needed;
- recommendations for training providers/suppliers;
- an estimate of costs (audit/consultancy fee, trainer's fee, estimated lost working time, examination fee, purchase of learning materials and hardware);
- the method of payment (budget code); and
- a statement of benefits for the company and the individual (contextualised within the corporate plan).

The supplier's specification

The second specification is a checklist of training issues for discussion with potential suppliers. It will ultimately form the contract specification for the supply of training on a medium- to long-term basis. It also provides you with a checklist of discussion points which relate to key aspects of the delivery: e.g. mode, method, location of training and learning goals – issues which will also have been raised in the language audit report.

Ask your prospective training company whether they would:

- arrange a one-hour sample class (for demo and quality control purposes);
- diagnose the linguistic aptitude of the trainees (='diagnostic entry test');
- group trainees according to level/ability;
- produce a written plan of the programme's design (schedule, duration and milestone learning goals);
- select training materials relevant to the company's needs;
- select a method in line with the individual's own preferences;
- incorporate 'open learning' for reinforcement;
- select trainers with a non-academic approach to teaching languages;
- monitor quality of training and learning regularly and systematically; and
- provide end-of-course assessment/preferably accredited certification.

The relevance of this for your company is to ensure the training provider prepares a fuller specification in advance and not simply an open agreement to carry out training. It also enables your company to monitor the training and lets the supplier know that your company expects a professional (rather than an *ad hoc*) service – i.e. a carefully constructed model of effective training geared directly to end-user requirements.

CHOOSING THE TRAINING SUPPLIER

What are the options?

There are three main models of language training structures (with variants) currently operating in companies that are worth considering:

   I in-company languages unit (a wholly owned in-house service unit of the company);

  II contract language service (an outside agency acting as the company's subcontractor for training); and

 III open-market provision (each requirement put out to tender).

Type I. In-company languages unit

Advantages:

- customised service;
- develops specialism in language training with experienced tutors and training materials;
- offers comprehensible integrated service (translation; interpreting; training);
- available for advice and verbal enquiries;
- 'friendly', 'homely' service on-site;
- popular with clients;
- shares company culture, organisation and goals; and
- can be profitable and may win extra business by marketing its services on the open market.

Disadvantages:

- fixed overheads (can be costly);
- requires complex round of budget-fixing with client departments;
- service difficult to cost (especially 'open-door' enquiries);
- can be difficult/costly to close down;
- requires attractive accommodation (which may not be in use all the time);
- requires management and clerical support (including receptionist);
- requires external monitoring to ensure quality service; and
- teaching approach and methods can ossify if service is 'ghettoised' within one company.

Type II. Contract language service

Advantages: can provide customised on-site service similar to above; your company can 'shop around' for best supplier; easy to terminate contract if performance unsatisfactory; contract renegotiable on annual or biennial basis.

Disadvantages: can be too profit-conscious; open-door policy may not operate for staff; may be less concerned with developmental work (e.g. materials development and tutor-training); does not share company culture; tutor turnover can be high; tutors may have temporary status and be unqualified; service still needs managing, budgeting and monitoring; non-standard certification system may be used.

Type III. Open-market provision

Advantages: cheapest solution for immediate need; you can 'shop around' and buy best match ('horses for courses'); no long-term commitment.

Disadvantages: quality can be highly variable and has to be taken on trust; no come-back; less likely to be adapted to company needs and culture; unlikely to be sound basis for an ongoing medium- to long-term strategy; course materials more likely to be 'general' (=less adapted to your specific needs).

Until recently, the first two types tended to exist only in the largest international companies (e.g. type I: ICI, Siemens, BASF, Thomson; type II: Peugeot Talbot (UK), Bayer), where they could provide company-specific service for translation, training and cultural briefing. Internationalisation of business has brought an increasing number of companies in the medium to large league like Norwich Union (UK) and Moet & Chandon (France) into type I. Type III has remained the most popular with smaller businesses for reasons of resource limitations.

The increasing growth of the specialist service sector has meant that your company is likely to be deluged with suppliers' literature once you make your intentions known either to subcontract your entire training needs over a period of time (type II) or simply to buy in a single training programme (type III).

Setting up your own languages unit will require specialist help. Some companies have done this almost by default by appointing a language trainer and giving him or her an office and tutorial room for classes. However, this kind of *ad hoc* approach can lead to major difficulties since the tutor is rarely a 'manager' and will experience problems setting up a centre without formal support from the company. In the long run, your company will do well to buy in a professional language training consultancy to plan the unit or centre if this is your preferred model. One tip would be to approach one of the existing in-company schemes and seek to commission them to advise you on how to do it.

Selecting a good supplier

Most companies will probably look first to a reputable supplier or established agency and either subcontract all the language training for a year or so, or simply commission the training on a one-off basis. In these cases, beware of assuming that *any* training agency, or management consultancy, can handle languages – most have never done so because this is a relatively new field of management development in this country and few genuine specialists exist. So be sure to check out their claims to be experienced and ask for a written breakdown of past clients, for whom they have managed language training or provided a language service.

It may also be interesting to ask to see the CV of any proposed consultant. The ideal consultant is usually a graduate who has been a language trainer in companies before (preferably qualified in teaching languages to adults) and who has had management experience in a similar language centre elsewhere. He or she may also have spent some time abroad – where this kind of experience is quite common. You may be surprised to discover that there are few people who have these credentials in the UK (though many may claim they can do the job!) and agencies or consultancies with household names that can legitimately claim to have worked in this field to any degree.

First invite two or three to meet you informally (before asking for formal quotations). Explain your company's (or the individual's) culture, needs and goals, ask them for their opinion on how they would structure the optimal training programme for your company. Go through the checklist in 'The Supplier's Specification' section (pages 55–6) and see how they respond. If necessary, bring in an independent languages consultant to join your panel. From their response and level of awareness of issues, including the principle of reaching needs-related learning goals (i.e. customised training, rather than implementing a fixed course of instruction), you will easily gauge their level of professionalism and willingness to adapt their product to your needs.

Buying a course of language training should be treated like every other purchase in business. In fact, buying training is far more complex than purchasing an item of equipment. Unless you carry out these planning stages systematically – or employ a consultant to do it for you – there is the inevitable risk that the expensive training will deteriorate into the old-fashioned teacher–pupil focus where the syllabus may, at worst, become whatever takes the teacher's fancy on the day! Business language training – with its emphasis on a tight timescale and tangible outcomes – has to be seen in quite a different light to learning French at school. The 'teacher' is a professional trainer and therefore no longer sole master of the classroom or the syllabus. The company or individual first have to identify what they want to get out of the training, what the limiting factors are (e.g. time constraints) and then require the training group to tailor-make an appropriate programme.

Above all, you will see whether the supplier is marketing a 'panacea programme' which will 'turn your trainees into linguists in less than 24 hours' – this may provide an interesting, alternative way of approaching language learning, but it will only exceptionally meet your corporate or individual goals.

When looking for a language training provider:

- seek independent advice;
- telephone other companies for their opinion;
- 'shop around' for different suppliers at home and abroad;
- ask for several quotes for different combinations of training;
- negotiate down the final unit price by asking for a complete package;
- ask for independent monitoring of training outcomes; and
- build flexible timing and delivery dates in to the training schedules.

When you have clarified any constraints on the training from your company's perspective, you will need to draw up written specifications of the possible options. The training specification will also tell you a great deal about the level of professionalism, knowledge and experience that the supplier has in the field of business language training. One of these versions will form the blueprint for the implementation stage.

IMPLEMENTING THE TRAINING SCHEME

'If you are going to set up a training scheme ... which says that Joe Bloggs will be doing language training on Friday afternoon from 3 pm to 6 pm, it is not going to work.'
(Richard Collinge, Chloride Industrial Batteries)

Implementing the language training programme means making decisions about *how, when, where, for whom, and by whom* the training should take place. Ideally, you should discuss the options with a languages consultant. But you will need to be aware of the parameters, constraints and conditions for effective learning that can influence the design (and ultimate success) of the course. No single model or approach is right for all companies and all people all of the time; in other words, there is no single panacea. Each company can, however, build up a customised training scheme which suits it from the component parts below. Broadly speaking, these can be divided into five bands of 'building blocks', over which you should be able to exercise choice:

- *course structure*:
  - mode (e.g. crash course or regular weekly; open learning or face to face); focus of content (e.g. balance of reading, writing, listening and reading skills; language *v.* culture); duration (e.g. timing and hours per week; length of course); evaluation – external exam/internal assessment;
- *learning environment*:
  - location (on-site or abroad; classroom-based or open learning – see chapters 4 & 5); atmosphere (positive/negative, etc.);
- *methodology* (or 'approach'):
  - 'traditional' (e.g. grammar-translation); audio-lingual (e.g. audio-visual); direct method (e.g. immersion); communicative (e.g. function and task-based); 'the latest' (e.g. stress-reducing methods; suggestopaedia); eclecticism (= a combination of all the above!);
- *learning technology*:
  - applications of hardware and software (e.g. printed material;

TV/video – audio & video cassettes, satellite broadcasts; use of self-access open learning centre; computer programs);
- *learner type*:
  - individual aptitude, motivation, attitude, personality, educational background (existing language skills); and
- *tutor type*:
  - personality, teaching technique, commitment, attitude, knowledge and experience, qualifications, background (nationality), quality of preparation.

How these fit together into models is best seen in examples currently operating in British companies:

Company 'A': A large variety of personnel need to learn languages; engineers, computer staff, secretaries, paint shop workers and accountants. Self-tuition language labs were found to be ineffective without a live tutorial system. Beginners are trained by English tutors, the more advanced by native-speakers. They now have 300 students in 65 classes – with a maximum of six to a group (though students argue that four gives them the right level of attention). Classes are grouped according to level of competence, but mixed as to status – though the MD has one-to-one instruction. Self-instruction was found to be weak because the material did not give enough explanation; crash courses were found to be 'shattering', but useful in that they replicated the situation that existed abroad. They are now experimenting with one-day intensives and regular visits to the country.

Company 'B': The staff needing language skills are sales and marketing, receptionists and telephonists. Before the course begins staff have to take a linguistic aptitude test; the training is in phases – progress is monitored by oral tests and course evaluation by questionnaire. The course structure is 2×2 hours' tuition per week in groups of seven – with an additional four hours' per week open learning – designed to fit round work. The open learning materials have been specially designed by a local college and are intended for reinforcement exercises. The company has its own highly rated open learning centre, containing a stock of material, including video and audio cassette material. Groups are mixed initially, then streamed. The problems identified by the company are: length of time required for training; staff availability; staff motivation (especially self-tuition); level of concentration; grouping of different levels and pace of learning. One-to-one was found to be an expensive method, over-dependent on good tutors. Open learning (in combination) was the way forward.

Company 'C': Intensive courses are organised for managers going abroad. Generally, they are one-to-one, but grouped where helpful. Cultural briefing is incorporated into the programme. The training is tightly focused on improving corporate profitability and the most cost-effective method is looked for. The company recruits personnel on the basis of their language skills and the language training policy is currently under review in the light of 'Single Europe'. The company sponsors employees to learn languages in evening class at the tech and provides open learning packages (but without tutorial support).

There are, first, overarching considerations of the company's budgetary constraints (in 'B'), the development of a formal training strategy (e.g. the 'policy' considerations in company 'C'), availability of open learning (in 'B') and the adherence to fixed corporate objectives (in 'C'). The companies have variously experimented with combinations of structure, methodology, timing, group size and composition (i.e. the selection and streaming of learners by aptitude) and types of tutor. 'A' rejects open learning, while 'B' has invested in an open learning centre that is, apparently, successful. Perhaps not surprisingly, each company has reached different conclusions on how the training model should be constructed – which suggests that *eclecticism* is the best approach, after all.

It is important to draw up a list of the possiblities (with your languages consultant), taking account of certain established patterns. For example, most companies prefer to set up language training on-site, rather than in a remote location so that key personnel are not missing for too long (though the personnel themselves do not always agree!). Group sizes vary, but the optimal size is usually no more than six or seven, otherwise the opportunity to speak is too limited. Some companies are strongly in favour of open learning methods, others against. The received view is that face-to-face tuition is the most effective when it is available, but the combination of classroom tuition dovetailed with tutor-led open learning can also be very effective when there are time constraints.

The table below provides an overview of the advantages and disadvantages of the timing and composition of classes, which are discussed in greater detail in chapters 4 and 6.

	PROS	**CONS**
SMALL GROUP CLASS	*group may provide:*	*individual may suffer from:*
	• more scope for interaction	• progress at pace of slowest
	• group dynamic	• less relevance to need
	• mutual support	• frequent absences in group
	• healthy competition	
	• cost-effectiveness	
	PROS	**CONS**
ONE-TO-ONE CLASS	*one-to-one classes may be:*	*individual may suffer from:*
	• self-pacing	• intensity (= stress)
	• more relevant	• over-exposure to trainer
	• faster	• lack of contact with others
	• more flexible in timing & content	• expense
	PROS	**CONS**
CRASH COURSE (25 + hrs per week)	*may:*	*may suffer from:*
	• *be effective as refresher*	• *intensity*
	• *be effective before going abroad*	• *rapid memory loss*
	• *concentrate the mind*	• *limited absorption after 30hrs a week*
	• *provide no distractions*	• *expense*
		• *absence of learner from work*
		• *need for frequent refreshers*

- *launch a total beginner*
- *be better for specific skills (e.g. reading course)*
- *provide sense of rapid progress*

	PROS	**CONS**
	may:	*may not work because:*
REGULAR WEEKLY (2–6 hrs per week)	• be more effective in long term • be effective for skill maintenance • improve absorption of learning • provide more flexible class times • provide choice of groups • limit absence from work • be booked on diary basis (one-to-one)	• most manage to attend only about half the classes • only the persistent survive • takes a long time to see 'real progress'

How long does it take to learn a foreign language?

There is, of course, no hard and fast rule about how long it takes to learn another language – it is rather like asking how long it will take someone to learn to drive a car. The answer depends on a host of factors – availability of good tutors, a well-designed, relevant programme, a comfortable environment, a client-centred approach, effective teaching and learning methods, corporate and family support, the student's existing level of linguistic skills and knowledge of other languages. Above all, there is personal *motivation*, which largely determines how many hours an individual commits to the programme, as well as the student's will to carry on when progress seems slow, or when other diversions compete with the little time that is available.

In brief, the major factors which will affect the individual's rate of learning are:

• individual commitment and motivation;

- knowledge of another foreign language;
- knowledge of a related language;
- self-study time available;
- teaching methods;
- class environment and size;
- quality, training and interest of tutors; and
- external distractions.

The US Foreign Service Institute's graphs of the levels of proficiency which adults can achieve in different languages show that the average English-speaker needs some 720 hours of classroom time to reach a point halfway between *minimal professional proficiency* and *working professional proficiency* from zero. They estimate that learners of harder languages, like Arabic, Chinese and Korean, require two to three times the number of hours to reach the same level as for European languages.

Great care has been taken when interpreting any figures on learning rates. In the past, for example, you were expected to achieve competence in all four skills – speaking, listening, reading and writing (with a greater emphasis on the latter two) – before you were deemed successful. However, most people in business only need a combination of two of these skills and a limited set of foreign words to fulfil 85% of their job. A good tutor will identify which skills and vocabulary are most needed and provide a shortened, highly focussed programme to meet them.

In your planning, though, you will need to formulate a rough idea of the cost of language training – which will depend entirely on the time required to reach a certain stage of competence in a given skill for a given individual in your company. The table on page 68, which is based on the Australian Department of Foreign Affairs and Trade's *Guide to Learning Rate*, will give you an approximate idea of the minimum time (hours of tuition) required to progress through three levels of language competence in the four major groups of languages – from the easiest (western and northern European) to the hardest (East Asian). 'Minimum hours tuition' is an estimate of the minimum time a linguistically gifted person would require; 'Maximum hours tuition' is the approximate figure for a less able linguist to reach the same level. A learner will need to spend at least as many hours per week in self-study, or in the language laboratory, as in face-to-face tuition, so this is added in brackets. In terms of costing the training, most agencies charge between £25 and £50 per hour for face-to-face tuition – with a smaller add-on cost for the use of an open-access language for self-study.

Description of levels

Level I: Student can meet basic survival needs; can get around, hold simple conversations, carry out transactions in shops, post offices, bars, etc., and read notices and give simple messages on familiar topics. Can express likes and dislikes, but speaks hesitantly and misunderstandings arise.

Level II: Student can speak well enough to meet routine practical and social demands and limited requirements of own particular business field. Can discuss work conditions, personal opinions and preferences. Can follow the gist of business meetings – but unable to follow fluent conversations overheard between native speakers.

Level III: Student can meet most practical and social demands and the basic requirements of own business field. Can participate in most formal and informal discussions; can make presentations to colleagues in a foreign language with 'broken fluency'. Can read technical reports in own field and understand standard newspaper stories addressed to the general reader.

The difference in time and cost between training the two learner types can be significant (i.e. up to two or three times greater), so evaluating a candidate's aptitude before signing an open-ended contract can be crucial. However, if you are uncertain of a person's aptitude, taking the average of the minimum and maximum hours for each stage will give you a general idea of the time required.

Can you spot good learners?

The quick answer is 'yes'. But, more importantly, you can profile a trainee's learning style so as to administer a better matched 'prescription' in the training programme. For example, it is possible to identify a potential fast-track language learner from interview, or possibly from certain entries in his or her CV.

Level
Speaking and reading levels (excluding 'writing')

	I	II	III
LANGUAGE GROUP I *Dutch, French, Italian, German, Portuguese, Spanish, Swedish*			
Min. hrs/tuition (+self-study)	75 (+75)	150 (+150)	270 (+270)
Max. hrs/tuition (+self-study)	210 (+210)	420 (+420)	750 (+750)
Average wks in Crash Course (@ 30 hrs per week)	7	14	26
LANGUAGE GROUP II *Farsi, Greek, Hindi, Urdu*			
Min. hrs/tuition (+self-study)	120 (+120)	225 (+225)	450 (+450)
Max. hrs/tuition (+self-study)	360 (+360)	660 (+660)	1320 (+1320)
Average wks in Crash Course (@ 30 hrs per week)	12	22	44
LANGUAGE GROUP III *Hebrew, Polish, Russian, Thai, Turkish, Vietnamese*			
Min. hrs/tuition (+self-study)	150 (+150)	270 (+270)	600 (+600)
Max. hrs/tuition (+self-study)	420 (+420)	750 (+750)	1800 (+1800)
Average wks in Crash Course (@ 30 hrs per week)	14	26	62
LANGUAGE GROUP IV *Arabic, Chinese, Japanese, Korean*			
Min. hrs/tuition (+self-study)	150 (+150)	450 (+450)	960 (+960)
Max. hrs/tuition (+self-study)	450 (+450)	1350 (+1350)	2850 (+2850)
Average wks in Crash Course (@ 30 hrs per week)	16	44	96

Checklist for spotting the 'fast track' language learner:

- already speaks the language well (just needs refresher);
- is well motivated, adaptable and 'into' self-development;
- has already studied the language (or is studying it in evening class);
- speaks other languages (i.e. has a 'gift');
- able to use own language well (e.g. understands how grammar rules work);
- is a good communicator and sociable;
- can mimic, put on 'funny voices' and play-act (likes amateur drama);
- is good at developing own learning strategies (i.e. can memorise 'odd' words easily);
- has close ties with the country (perhaps married to national, or has lived there);
- likes the country, its people and its culture;
- likes travelling and meeting people.

A number of language training suppliers, for example, carry out linguistic aptitude tests to identify not only the best potential language learners, but also the estimated rate of learning of a key employee who *has to learn* a particular language. Aptitude tests can also be designed to identify whether, and how effectively, a potential learner can use learning strategies either to speed up his or her memory processes or to find out more about the new language. This will produce a picture of how effective the individual's learning style is. The training method can then be adjusted to the individual learner more readily.

Can you improve learning rates?
The evidence on successful language learning supports the intro-duction of language learning strategies into the training prog-ramme: i.e. students should be taught how to develop their own strategies because:

- there is a link between the use of language learning strategies and successful performance;
- trainees who develop learning strategies can take greater responsibility for their own learning; and
- learners can be trained to use learning strategies.

Good language learners employ a range of effective learning strategies: for example, they

- consciously develop a range of visual mnemonic, rhyming and other association devices to memorise foreign words and expressions;
- rapidly become pro-active in the learning process;
- prefer to drive the learning process themselves;
- carefully listen and check information themselves;
- show eagerness to practise and communicate with others;
- think first in the foreign language (without seeking support from English);
- actively try to use the language in meaningful situations;
- test their learning by practising out loud, unafraid to make errors;
- find alternative ways of saying things without simplification; and
- monitor their own output, repeating the correct version over to self.

By copying these strategies, language learners can improve their learning rate substantially – speeding up the time it takes to learn the language. For example, someone with a 'good memory' – i.e. system for memorising – who can remember new foreign words and structures has a distinct advantage. In conversation, most Europeans tend to use a small basic stock of about 2000 words for most of their everyday non-specialist communication. Learning words is not the same as learning a language, but if done systematically over time it can dramatically speed up the language learning process. For example, if a person were to learn only 10 foreign words a day, he or she would have the basic core vocabulary for a European language in about six months!

Different people, of course, learn in different ways and employ different strategies. Older people, for example, and those with a traditional educational background, often feel happier with a course which emphasises the structure of the language, or uses the grammar as a platform on which to introduce and practise new language. This is because they already have an awareness of the 'building bricks' of language from their first language, which they then use to 'build' the new one. New language needs to be 'attached', or 'hooked on', to existing knowledge – it is then better absorbed and more likely to stay in the long-term memory. A good tutor will take account of the trainee's existing knowledge and linguistic skills when deciding on a method and choosing the material.

However, it is important to realise that today there has never been a better range of methods and materials to choose from when you decide to start a language. If you are a paying customer, you can expect to discuss with your tutor what might be the best teaching method, style, learning approach and materials to suit your particular need and purpose.

Can you spot good tutors?

Most good tutors in Britain tend to be either modern language graduates or native speakers who are English graduates in their own country. Many will have spent some time in industry and gained at least three years' experience of training or teaching adults, preferably abroad. If they are British, they should have a teaching qualification like the well-respected RSA Diplomas in Teaching English as a Foreign Language, or Teaching Foreign Languages to Adults, which emphasise teaching languages for practical communication. Some excellent tutors have also come out of industry – rather than education – and have an acute insight into the business need which requires a language solution. In this case, however, you have to be sure that they are *linguistically* competent, as well as able to teach. One tip is to ask the prospective tutor to teach a demonstration lesson – this, above all else, will decide the matter!

Many companies employ native speakers directly, without going to a training supplier. Most people prefer to be taught by a national of the country – it makes good sense and brings the flavour and culture of the country into the classroom. Some native speakers, however, are unable to teach their own language and cannot explain its structure adequately. So you will need to check whether he or she can actually teach in a way that suits your company's goals. After all, how many British business people could walk into a foreign classroom tomorrow and explain why we say 'I'd rather you *didn't* do that!' (using the past tense about the future) in preference to 'I'd rather you *won't* do that!'?

MEASURING AND EVALUATING OUTCOMES

'My Chairman and Managing Director are always ringing me up asking if this training is actually profitable. It is difficult to prove, but one of the things that we have noticed over the past six months is that we have won a number of major orders and our business expansion plans seem to be going to schedule. But what I am finding from the sales and marketing people is that they have more confidence.' (Richard Collinge, Chloride Industrial Batteries)

'Managers at Fujitsu's small British subsidiary who took training in Japanese succeeded in persuading their head office to buy ICL, thereby shifting Fujitsu's centre of European operations from Germany to the UK.' (*The Independent*, 30 May 1991)

Ensuring value for money

Above all, the ultimate success of the training will be judged with reference to:

- results; and
- return on investment.

Certification of results

The results of the training programme should be measurable against the original specification agreed with the trainer and reported in a certificate issued by the supplying company. Better still, the trainees should sit an externally moderated examination in order to ensure quality control. The student will then receive a certificate which also has some career value with the stamp of a recognised exam body.

Nowadays, some extremely flexible examination schemes exist which can be used to certificate most training programmes; the most popular business language examination schemes in British companies are those of the London Chamber of Commerce (LCCI), the Royal Society of Arts (RSA) and the Institute of

Linguists (IoL). The City and Guilds Institute of London (CGLI) also developed a highly flexible and innovative framework of 'content-free' vocational language schemes in 1991 which the supplier can match with the specific skills required in his or her industry.

The advantages for your company of incorporating external examinations is that they will verify the levels attained and the certificate they issue will have greater credibility than the supplier's own. More important, the existence of the new industry standards issued by the Languages Lead Body and now incorporated into the National Vocational Qualification (NVQ) framework of language standards (with prospective European transfer and accreditation) means that the learner will have a piece of paper which indicates that he or she has reached a certain level of competence in the language and has acquired certain skills. The kind of levels envisaged for certification and the description of competencies will be similar to those set out in the 'Speaking and reading levels' table on page 68. So employers will know what an individual can *actually do* with a foreign language at work.

Whatever the face value of the end-of-course certificate, it should list the tasks which the individual can perform after undergoing the training. While the newly acquired competencies are spelt out for each individual in tailor-made certificates (see page 74), you should also be able to see at a glance how well the final performance checks off against the original training goals in the specification.

The supplier's report

The supplier's report on the programme should add extra information, highlighting individual achievements, identifying gaps and any practical difficulties and making recommendations for further action. The report should also provide an evaluation of the student's performance against the original training goals. If you are still uncertain about whether these goals have been reached, you may also need to bring in an independent assessor to test the students. On the other hand, the most cost-effective way for your company to ensure quality control is to incorporate some form of externally assessed exam or test near, or at, the end of the

Date:

CERTIFICATE OF PROFICIENCY IN SPANISH TELEPHONE SKILLS

This is to certify that Mr/Mrs/Ms .... has successfully completed a Beginners/Intermediate/ Advanced (delete) training course in Spanish Telephone Skills. The course was conducted from ..... (date) to ..... (date) in .... (place) and consisted of ..... hours' classroom tuition and ..... hours' open learning.

At the end of the training Mr/Mrs/Ms .... (the trainee) was able to liaise with callers and handle the following operations:

- receive and initiate telephone calls
- transfer callers to the appropriate personnel
- request caller's details and make a written note of them
- explain reasons for absence of a manager
- pass on messages to callers
- take down simple messages involving spelling names, time, location and measurement
- comprehend, identify the nature of non-technical enquiries concerning:
  - the company's products
  - orders and invoices
  - quantity and price
  - despatch, shipment and distribution of goods
  - credit terms

The training programme was conducted by .... Ltd, and the tutor was .... The end of course test was conducted by ....

Signed

programme. If it is inconvenient to hold a comprehensive exam, a simple oral test may do, such as the London Chamber of Commerce's 'FLIC' test, which can be administered anywhere at any time on demand and will serve broadly to verify the student's level.

The ultimate assessment is not whether the objectives of the training have been reached, but whether there has been any *return on the investment*. Although this is far more problematic to quantify, the training should have some impact on your company's performance and ideally should be measurable in terms of growth, profitability and/or penetration of new international markets, or greater efficiency at the departmental level.

The impact of a language training programme on company profit can be particularly difficult to measure unless there has been some dramatic improvement or breakthrough which cannot be attributed to any cause other than language training. The case of ICL and Fujitsu is, however, an exception to this. Similarly, Chloride Industrial Batteries estimates a 60% increase in its sales to Europe after training 5% of its employees in French and German – although the concurrent export drive in Europe was also a factor.

The benefits for the individual, on the other hand, can be immediate. In the follow-up questionnaire at Chloride Industrial Batteries, 80% of those doing French claimed it was 'directly relevant' to their job; German – 50% 'relevant' to their job; while *all* receptionists (100%) – i.e. those at the point of first contact – felt it was 'immediately relevant'. However, unless you ensure that there is a system for evaluating the later impact of the training on company performance in the follow-up strategy, the company will be less likely to finance training for very long.

FOLLOWING UP

The first phase of the follow-up is, of course, to evaluate whether the linguistic deficiencies pinpointed by the audit have been rectified. The second phase is to build language training into your company's medium- to long-term plans as part of HRD. Achieving both the short-term evaluative goal in the first phase and the long-term developmental objective in the second require a further series of steps:

Short-term follow-up:
- evaluation reports on training to be submitted by trainers and trainees separately;
- trainees to receive certificate of their language competencies;
- training outcomes matched against goals;
- external language assessor to test trainees' language skills (if necessary);
- performance of trainees on the job to be monitored regularly to assess level of improvement;
- certificate to be copied to personnel file;
- progress of trainees to be monitored six months after training; and
- refresher or continuation courses to be encouraged.

Longer-term follow-up:
- setting up a three-year language and culture training strategy;
- drafting of a formal language training policy;
- development of a database of staff with language skills by Personnel;
- project to write company-specific language training materials;
- setting up of an in-company languages unit, or open learning centre *with tutorial support*;
- closer working relationship with a training provider;
- changes to personnel policy (e.g. hiring of nationals, or more secondments);
- recruitment of staff with language skills; and
- inclusion of language skills in adverts for jobs.

In many British and American companies, language training needs have traditionally been dealt with in an *ad hoc* manner, whereas a number of the leading Continental firms accept language training and cultural briefing as a major part of human resource development, designed to achieve long-term international growth. Launching a programme of efficient language training requires the development of an ongoing strategy not only to maintain the level of skills acquired, but also to ensure business growth beyond the short term. But an effective policy of foreign language and culture training is only possible where it is integrated within a broader HRD strategy to internationalise the company culture through a programme of training and development. Language training is one of a series of ways forward – but the success of its implementation depends on the chemistry of its separate parts, which is analysed in the following chapters.

Checklist of main steps towards an integrated training strategy

- evaluate 'cultural receptivity' of company;
- engage languages consultant;
- identify and allocate responsibilities for actioning solution within company;
- calculate real cost of training in human resources, time and training fees;
- locate budget;
- survey language training needs at corporate, departmental, job, individual and task level;
- translate language needs into corporate and individual training goals;
- ensure that course content, methods, schedule, technology meet training objectives;
- ensure that language training scheme takes account of capabilities and preferences of individual trainees: (i) previous experience of languages, (ii) linguistic aptitude, (iii) timing, and (iv) location;
- select flexible, qualified, language trainer;
- check that trainees' performance is monitored;
- ensure course outcomes are certificated; and
- try to develop idea of language training as part of international HRD strategy.

TQM criteria apply to language training, too, so think:

- end user;
- professionalism;
- clearly defined targets;

- cost-effectiveness;
- a service product in the company;
- client orientation;
- quality;
- accountability; and
- results.

———————————

CHAPTER FOUR

FACE-TO-FACE TUITION

DOUG EMBLETON

FACE-TO-FACE TUITION FOR ADULTS

• Memories of 'the classroom' • Where does it fit within the training programme? • A balanced diet

FACE-TO-FACE TUITION FOR BUSINESS

• Who are the learners? • Who are the tutors? • When learners meet tutors

FACE-TO-FACE TUITION FOR ADULTS

Memories of 'the classroom'

Many of us have a preconceived idea of what to expect from 'classroom' tuition in a foreign language. These preconceived ideas are referred to in chapter 1 and are normally based on our negative experiences of language learning from our schooldays. They can be a barrier to successful language learning for adults.

However, there are fundamental differences between these experiences and the realities of successful language training for adults.

As a first step towards eliminating this potential barrier we should replace the term 'classroom' with the term 'face-to-face tuition'.

Where does it fit within the training programme?

As we have seen in chapter 3, which examines the range of existing routes towards successful in-company or business language training, face-to-face tuition has a pivotal role to play. Indeed, the case studies provided by Norwich Union, Lloyds of London and ICI Chemicals & Polymers (see chapter 14) provide real-life confirmation that face-to-face tuition is the cornerstone of an effective language training programme in a business context. The case studies also give checklists of good practice and the need to use language teachers trained to teach adults.

Chapter 6 ('crash courses') provides a practical insight into that particular type of face-to-face tuition and other chapters examine the equally important roles of self-tuition, computer-assisted language learning, TV and video, self-tuition and language training materials as consolidation elements of the learning process.

A balanced diet

The key message, therefore, is that a *balanced diet* of all that is good from the range of training possibilities covered in this book is the best approach. This message is reaffirmed in each individual chapter. None of the individual methods of language training claims to be a 'stand-alone' or 'all-in-one' solution and this underlies the concept of an integrated language training strategy for business. However, it can be justifiably claimed that within the balanced diet of language training, face-to-face tuition should invariably constitute the main course and that the other components should constitute the accompanying wines, hors d'oeuvres and dessert.

Face-to-face tuition only succeeds as the cornerstone of a language training programme if the student is willing to pay for (in terms of time and commitment) and digest other courses on the menu. Language learning is not achieved in the classroom alone and consolidation and practice are equally vital to the learning process.

FACE-TO-FACE TUITION FOR BUSINESS

Who are the learners?

I must say that in my 20 years' experience of developing language training for business I have been unable to define a *typical* learner. In fact, one of the inherent dangers when implementing any language training programme within an organisation is to excessively stereotype the categories of learners both in terms of their function and in terms of their status within the organisation.

A prominent feature of many of the messages transmitted by the bandwagon of '1992' was a doom and gloom scenario that exports and sales would be drastically affected as a result of the perceived lack of language skills in British industry and commerce. Undoubtedly, this message has more than a ring of truth to it but one has to look a long way behind the stereotyped concept of sales and exports in order to confront the real issue of *who* should be learning languages. Just as is the case with slick phrases used to advertise 'panacea' solutions to language training, the exhortation messages for business in the '1992' context had a limiting but undeniably effective net result. They implanted a picture in people's minds of language skills being somehow restricted to sales and export functions.

This is far from true. One mental picture is of export salesmen metaphorically 'parachuting' into overseas markets, winning contracts and orders and bringing these back to the UK. The rationale is that they will successfully negotiate in the language of the overseas market and will thus be living proof of the need for language skills.

The concept of the integrated language strategy, which is the main theme of this book, immediately dispels this notion. If sales and export functions were the only recipients of language training this would mean that the overseas order would be subsequently handled and processed by an organisation which, apart from its elite overseas sales force, had remained totally *unintegrated* with the many, many other foreign language requirements engendered by overseas markets and orders.

Apart from verbal communications in foreign languages, overseas markets will naturally create the need for efficient translation services and foreign language advertising because communication with overseas markets assumes all shapes and forms. These functions will be carried out by professional linguists. So, who are the learners who will benefit from face-to-face tuition and, in particular, from acquiring communicative, spoken skills in a foreign language?

The following cameos are derived from my own experience and will obviously be different in other organisations. They do, however, clearly illustrate the increasingly wide range of jobs and functions at all levels of an organisation which contribute to, and play an extremely positive role within, the daily business/effectiveness of an organisation.

John Carrol works in the Security Department and is the uniformed gateman at the main entrance to the factory. As overseas orders have increased so has the incoming traffic of heavy goods vehicles which arrive to collect products from the factory. Joe has always had an interest in languages and other cultures and used to feel rather inadequate when he was unable to deal with even the most basic of requests from incoming drivers. He has now been attending a weekly, in-company German class for two years and has also brushed up his 'O' level French by using audio materials and books from the Learning Centre. The majority of incoming drivers speak either German or French and Joe has become well known amongst the drivers for his friendly and helpful service. He has to solve their problems by communicating directly in their own language.

Anna Lawrence works in the Export Department on the South American 'desk'. Although she is relatively junior in grade and does not travel to the South American markets, her desk is one of the focal points of contact for South American customers. For 15 months, Anna has been attending the weekly Spanish class specially designed for the small team in which she works. Her skills and confidence are gradually increasing and she can now handle some of the telephone calls from South America with confidence and to the great delight of the people making the call. Her involvement with the South American desk, even though it does not yet involve overseas travel, is much more meaningful. In time, as her career develops, she hopes to use her language skills more and more.

Ron Higgs is the Production Manager of a plant which produces a wide range of formulations of a raw material for the plastics industry. The company has now established a similar production capacity in France and Ron needs to attend regular meetings in France to coordinate product specifications and to pass on his production and engineering knowledge to his new French colleagues. He has not got enough time for the 'slow-drip' approach of a weekly two hour class but he is also too heavily involved with his production and managerial duties to attend a residential course. Flexibly timed face-to-face tuition on a one-to-one basis has been arranged in-house. Ron only has a three-minute journey from his place of work to his lesson. His 'O' level French was not quite as low a starting point as he had feared and the rapport with his tutor is excellent. They are now also able to use authentic materials from Ron's visits to France in order to focus part of the training on his real job requirements.

Kath Brown joined the company as Laboratory Supervisor and as her experience in her particular range of products increased so did the overseas market for the product in question. Kath has worked for the past 18 months in a troubleshooting role with German customers. She is ideally suited to this as she can relate to the problems of the customer's own technical and laboratory staff and can quickly translate the customer's problem not only linguistically but also technically. Previously, the after-sales problems were discussed by the customer's representatives and a sales person from Kath's company. However, this proved unsatisfactory as Kath would then have to interpret the salesperson's 'non-technical' view of the customer's problem before taking any action. Kath attended a weekly class for one year but then found the need to consolidate her

German skills through a combination of in-house one-to-one tuition, self-tuition videos and audio cassettes and two separate weeks of a crash course. She is delighted with her increasing ability to relate her technical skills to the immediate needs of overseas customers. So are the customers – whose technical requirements are now handled very promptly.

This series of cameos is, in my experience, merely the tip of the iceberg. Another way of addressing the issue is:

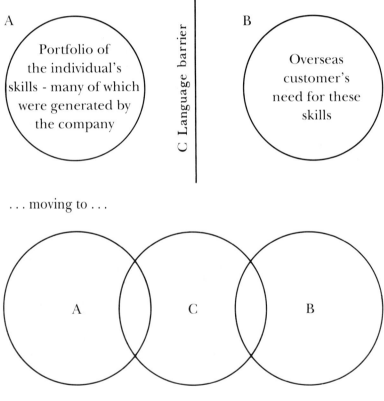

... whereby the individual is given every assistance to eliminate the language barrier and thereby apply his or her full portfolio of technical skills to the benefit of the overseas customers and to the organisation which he or she serves. It makes a lot of sense because the organisation has *already* invested a lot of time and money in enabling the individual to build up a portfolio of primary business and technical skills. Once there is an overseas dimension, the language barrier can almost totally negate and marginalise the skills portfolio of the individual.

- In all of these cases, face-to-face tuition has been the corner-stone of the language training process.
- The individuals concerned have consolidated their learning by using additional materials.
- Learners come from a range of functions and levels within the organisation.

Who are the tutors?

The in-company language training schemes described in chapter 14 all stress the same basic points in terms of the teachers or tutors who provide the language training.

- They are trained to teach adults.
- The content of each class is varied and includes relevant material which supplements the coursebook which the group or individual are following.
- Students are encouraged to speak and participate fully in a teaching atmosphere and environment specifically designed for adult learners.

It is inappropriate to include a profile of the 'perfect tutor'. For example, we are told elsewhere in this book that native speakers are not necessarily the best teachers (of their own language). Also, Norwich Union and Lloyd's of London, who recently established in-company language training, quite rightly placed an emphasis on recruiting people who were trained to teach adults.

Language tutors may be obtained from various sources which include:

- direct recruitment as individual (part-time) providers to in-company language training schemes where the in-company coordinator is a linguist;
- buying in from a specialist language training company; and
- buying in from a local college.

When buying in any language training services a useful tip is to speak with the coordinator or manager of the services about such things as how the tutors are trained, what previous or current experience they have of providing language training to business, success stories and positive outcomes of language training. In a nutshell, they also need to be able to speak another language – the language of business. If you have any residual doubts it really does pay to seek advice from a language consultant.

When learners meet tutors

One of the greatest pleasures of managing in-company language training is to see people make progress and derive practical benefits from their burgeoning language skills. Equally pleasurable is to know, simply by 'walking the corridor' and observing, that the same people are enjoying the actual learning process. Enjoyment and laughter are important parts of the process.

In order to achieve these two converging objectives, selection of the right teachers is vital. The return to what is perceived by many learners as 'the classroom' can induce an initial level of anxiety which only a skilled language trainer can detect and allay. Indeed, this anxiety could well be one of the major reasons for the constant recycling of the doom and gloom scenarios and reports of the shortage of language skills in British business. People tend to avoid things or situations which induce anxiety. It is much easier to write reports about them!

The environment in which the face-to-face tuition takes place is very important. For financial and logistical reasons, many organisations much prefer to accommodate any face-to-face tuition of the non-residential, intensive type on their own premises. For groups of students, a classroom 'eyes to the front' furniture setting simply will not do. The training room will facilitate eye contact, cross-table discussion and participation; it should be well equipped with items such as TV/video and audio equipment. Posters and maps related to other countries and languages will further enhance the learning environment by creating the right atmosphere.

Language learners in UK business need all of the encouragement and support that linguists can give them. As we see time and time again in this book, the emphasis has to be on 'Quality'. The end results of 'Quality' language training are of immeasurable benefit. Good face-to-face tuition is the cornerstone of this process.

CHAPTER FIVE

SELF-TUITION

STEPHEN HAGEN

WHAT IS SELF-TUITION?
• Can you really teach yourself a foreign language? • Types of self-tuition.

OPTIONS FOR SELF-TUITION
• Ingredients for effective self-tuition

WHAT IS SELF-TUITION?

Many business people who want to start a language are often attracted to the idea of self-tuition. Superficially, at least, it appears to be a panacea method: it is entirely flexible; you can start and break off when it suits you; you can commit as much or as little time as you like to teaching yourself the language; you do not have to attend classes at inconvenient times; you learn at your own pace at the times and in the manner you yourself determine, whether it is a personal stereo on a train, or simply reading a coursebook in an armchair.

Can you really teach yourself a foreign language?

Unfortunately, the answer is a resounding 'no' for the majority of people. Only a few people have the time, self-discipline and learning skills necessary to teach themselves a language for any length of time. Morever, there is a lack of good self-tuition materials, particularly in 'rarer' languages like Portuguese, Swedish or Russian. Without either a tutor, or adequate commercially available course materials, it is perhaps not surprising that the odds against succeeding are high. A recent survey of language training in business found that only one in five 'self-learners' felt they were successful at it.

When teaching themselves a language, particularly from scratch, the overwhelming majority of people are only able to work spasmodically and ineffectually at best and need guidance and feedback from a tutor. It seems only a few can be successful self-directed language learners. Provided the time commitment is there, the most effective form of language training is undoubtedly regular face-to-face tuition. Nonetheless, when there is no alternative, there are a number of ways in which self-tuition can be made a more enjoyable, purposeful and efficient learning experience within an integrated training programme.

Why choose self-tuition at all?

Although the arguments weigh strongly against self-tuition, many business people still turn to it as the only way of dealing with an otherwise intractable problem. They are either unable to attend classes regularly due to commitments at work or at home, or they cannot reach their desired language learning goals fast enough on the course available. Moreover, if they want to learn an exotic language like Japanese, Thai, Mandarin or Korean – all of which are increasingly important to British business – their chances of finding a course running nearby at a level and at a time that suits them are very low and, at present, qualified private tutors are few and far between. In this situation, they could either opt for a crash course (if the need is urgent and they have the time off and support of the company), or they can investigate self-tuition as a serious alternative.

Despite the trends, some people *do* succeed with self-tuition. Below are three examples of professional and business people who have embarked on one of the many and varied types of 'DIY' self-tuition programmes that are becoming increasingly popular with language learners who are unable to attend regular classes.

Three examples from business

A senior sales executive

Following a merger, Sheila Dunbar increasingly had to make trips to Italy to attend regular meetings with the senior managers of the Italian parent company. She felt well-disposed to learning Italian, but her schedule was too unpredictable for her to register for regular classes. She could not even guarantee her availability for an intensive course (and had to cancel two previously arranged courses through no fault of her own). Moreover, she is reluctant to eat into her own precious social life by going on a one-week residential course three times a year (during which time her work would pile up all the same, anyway!). Instead, she opted for a self-tuition course with cassettes and videos. She also installed a satellite TV receiver that would pick up Italian programmes (more for the romantic films than anything else). She manages to snatch some time here and there either travelling between meetings by car (and listening to the tapes) or on the train going home, when she can glance through the coursebook. Despite the irregularity, she is encouraged to continue because her few words of Italian have already greatly impressed her Italian colleagues and helped to create a much friendlier atmosphere during her visits to Italy. Her Italian colleagues have even started helping her with pronunciation. There is now the prospect of a more highly paid job in Italy if she can bring her Italian up to a level approaching fluency. So she has redoubled her efforts!

An engineer

Ian Tindle is a software engineer in a small company that specialises in customising business information systems. His company has acquired a grant from the British government to step up a distributor network in eastern Germany. As he was the only employee in the company to have done any German at school, he was asked to scan any e-mail, letters, or faxes that were expected to arrive in German in increasing numbers before passing them on to a qualified translator where necessary. The field reports from Dresden, which are always written in German, now arrive every week by fax. He decided he *had* to brush up his German and, since he has a young family with evening commitments, he has convinced his company to invest in a £1500 interactive video (IV). His company – a software development house – aggreed because it was culturally more receptive to hi-tech purchases than paying for lessons. The IV pack came with a self-study guide, worksheets and a telephone 'helpline', where at certain times he can reach a 'distance learning tutor', hired by the IV company to provide support. He finds this a far better medium than language labs or books and he is beginning to understand spoken German again very quickly. However, he feels he needs assistance with understanding written German – even at the mundane level of simple grammar – and he is also investigating computer-assisted language learning software for German.

An accountant
James Foreman is keen on languages and took French and Russian A level at school. He believed his career prospects would be enhanced if he could learn Spanish as well. His company did not see any business reason for paying for his training programme, so he had to decide between self-tuition in the company's open learning centre or a Spanish evening class at the local college. When he joined the evening class, he found the pace too slow and the other students more interested in casual 'holiday' Spanish than business Spanish. Already a speaker of a similar Romance language (i.e. French), he reckoned he could make faster progress on his own in the right environment. So he joined the local college's open-access language centre, where, for a small annual subscription of £60 (which his company finally agreed to pay), he could negotiate a short programme of tuition (15 minutes per consultation per week) and follow a course selected by the tutor specifically to meet his needs. He was able to use a variety of tapes and materials to back up his main coursebook. He also had access to Spanish satellite TV, which he watches for pleasure. Every three months, he now joins a residential weekend class organised by the tutor at the local college.

All three have found a combination of self-learning that suits their individual needs, circumstances and learning styles. They may not have found the ideal, or the best training solution, but they have developed a model to match their own personal, and their company's, limitations. Each of the three is currently succeeding because they each have a good reason for continuing and are well motivated. Either they have been spurred on by the prospect of improving their job prospects, or through experiencing a stimulating new technology, or they enjoy managing their own learning programme in a controlled environment.

Types of self-tuition

Self-tuition can take as many forms as there are self-learners. Each is distinguished by the degree to which the student has total control over the programme, ranging from the more open, but less effective 'autonomous', or 'traditional', self-tuition with no tutor and no outside advice, to the less open, but more effective 'supported self-study' – where a tutor is involved, but not in a direct teaching role. The three broad bands are described below.

- *Traditional self-tuition* is practised by Sheila Dunbar. It is the simplest form; it requires little technology (a coursebook, with or without cassettes) and learning can be carried out anywhere at any time, without reference to any external tutor. This is the most open and autonomous form of self-tuition. It is also the type least likely to succeed because of the sense of isolation and lack of feedback associated with it. On the other hand, Sheila has supplemented it with live surrogate tutors, her Italian colleagues, which has increased her chances of success substantially.
- *Distance learning* is where the learner is physically distant from a tutor, as on a correspondence course. Ian Tindle, for example, is following a form of distance learning by teaching himself from a self-study guide and an IV disc. A 'remote' tutor is available at the end of a telephone if needed. Ian Tindle could carry out his self-tuition programme equally well at home, unlike James Foreman, which implies it is more 'open' than the latter's.

- *Supported self-study*: James Foreman's model is a managed, or supported, self-learning programme where tutorial support is available on demand, but where there are certain restrictions, such as the opening times and availability of a tutor. His programme is negotiated with a tutor (whether it is for only 15 minutes' tuition a week or three hours), and he uses the full range of technology available in an open-access language centre, where, for example, he can 'drop' in after work. Rather like a doctor's surgery, he can make an arrangement to see his tutor by filling in a slot on the timetable in the centre. This is a less open form of learning, since a conscious attempt is made to match provision (including tutorial support, facilities, technology and materials) to learning need and learner preferences.

At one end of the scale, it involves simply buying a book in a shop, reading it and perhaps listening to the accompanying cassettes in isolation. At the other, there is a prescribed workplan, which has been agreed, designed, developed and customised by a languages specialist, which draws on a range of materials, technology, self-testing and client-led tutoring on demand. Supported self-study is, because of its 'flexible learning' approach, easily the most effective in the self-tuition, or open learning model, since it usually takes place in a tutor-controlled discrete language learning environment, like the open access language centre.

OPTIONS FOR SELF-TUITION

There is a number of self-tuition packages on offer, ranging from 'stand-alone' materials to self-access programmes in language centres. The self-learner can either opt for one of the three types below, or devise a combination of all of them.

The 'off-the-shelf' self-tuition pack

This basically comprises a coursebook with, or without, supplementary materials like audio or video cassettes, worksheets, self-evaluation tests, even computer programs, and/or a set of video tapes with a supplementary study guide. In this group you also have the interactive video disc, which is meant to contain all the 'supplementary materials' within it in the form of hypercards.

Many materials claim to be self-instructional, but this may just mean that they have a key to the exercises. Above all they should suit your purpose; e.g. if you want to learn to *speak* the language, there should be accompanying tapes; if you prefer a grammar-translation approach, check that there are plentiful grammatical explanations.

In the range of commercially produced printed materials, some are more focused on structures in the language and grammatical explanations. Others are geared towards 'survival' language and may be little more than expanded phrasebooks. In other words, choosing materials is rather like buying a new car; some buyers want to know about performance and appearance; others are far more interested in the engine and want to know what goes on under the bonnet. Choice of learning materials should match learner type. Whichever way you decide should influence your choice of course material. In brief, make sure that the materials contain a clear introduction for the self-learner, indicating the course objectives, content, skills, balance, level and target learner. A range of materials has been produced for the self-learner to supplement the basic coursebook, which can appear either in the main body of the book or as separate publications – e.g. guides on how to learn a language; workbooks; grammar notes; self-assessment, or progress, tests; revision exercises; culture and country guides. When scanning the available material, make sure you look at the full range of materials in the set to see how extensively it will meet your particular needs.

If in doubt, seek the recommendation of a languages consultant, or drop in to your local language centre at the poly, or college, scan the materials there and ask for advice and recommendations on what to buy.

Open/distance learning

The Open-University style of learning (course materials, 'remote' tutor, TV/video support, telephone contact) is unusual for language learning in the UK, but there are increasing opportunities with commitments from the Open Polytechnic and the Open University to teach languages at a distance and develop specialised distance-learning materials with extensive media applications. The advent, and convergence, of electronic mail, broadcast satellite TV from abroad, video conferencing and the multimedia networking envisaged in the proposed EC project, 'Eloquent', create many possibilities for innovation in foreign language distance learning in the future. At present, however, the field is limited to correspondence courses, telephone tutoring and help-lines linked to computer programs.

A number of language centres in polytechnics and universities offer a telephone (and call-in) subscriber service, where, for an annual fee, you can telephone your enquiry in and obtain advice and teaching assistance on a foreign language matter. Some colleges and commercial companies are also beginning to offer a regular telephone tutoring service where the client pays for a 20 minute telephone lesson, organised two to three times a week early in the morning. This can be a valuable support, especially when enthusiasm starts to flag.

At the other end of the technology spectrum, there is Ian Tindle's hi-tech approach – the sophisticated interactive 'multi-media' IV training system, where you can see, hear and 'feel' the foreign country, and communicate with a distance tutor either over a modem or by voice telephone. Increasingly, self-tuition in languages will involve this kind of hi-tech 'talking-computer', but at present the cost is prohibitive, the technical standard of the mass market still uncertain and there is not enough high quality commercial software on the market.

The open access language centre

Given the time constraints on many people, learning a language flexibly in an open access language centre (OALC) is a popular second-best to following a course of classroom-based face-to-face tuition. It is also popular. For example, Newcastle Polytechnic's OALC, 'Telelang', has some 500 part-time 'self-learners' who register each year and spend from an hour a fortnight to 20 hours a week studying there. About a quarter are business users, or those with career motivation. Most OALCs are housed in colleges, polys and universities.

Successful language learning in an OALC is often determined by the ease of access to its resources; the range of extra services on offer; the amenability and expertise of staff; and the range and 'user-friendliness' of available technology. OALCs can vary in size from a room with a few cassette recorders and a VCR tucked away at the top of a non-descript college building to a suite of carpeted, custom-designed rooms offering a range of hi-tech equipment, satellite/video material, live foreign TV and radio, well-catalogued material with a resident manager and helpful librarian. Some centres offer tutorial support for specific languages at set times, including early morning and twilight sessions.

Some are run on a commercial footing offering a range of services to business (e.g. customised audio, video and paper materials for business; training; interpreting; translation; briefings; business language examinations; and so on). They range, in approach, from the high quality and professional to the low budget and amateurish. Care should also be taken when considering any of the business services on offer, particularly translation and interpreting (see chapter 11).

Ingredients for effective self-tuition

The fast track learner profile outlined in chapter 3 applies equally here. Above all, a 'self-learner' needs staying power. Plodders seem to do better than sprinters at self-tuition. In the long run, self-discipline, habit formation and stamina count more than the initial upsurge of interest. The ingredients you will need for success include:

At the personal level:
• personal motivation;
• support from home and work;
• good time management;
• a set workplan; and
• clear objectives to work towards.

In the learning environment:
• relevant and stimulating material;
• suitable 'user-friendly' technology;
• tutor availability to answer questions and offer advice; and
• access to an OALC, if available.

CHAPTER SIX

CRASH COURSES

DIEGO GARCIA LUCAS

WHY A CRASH COURSE?
- Advantages and disadvantages

CAN YOU MEASURE STANDARDS AND QUALITY?
- Reducing the risk of poor results

SETTING REALISTIC OBJECTIVES
- Where it can go wrong • Where it can go right

PROBLEMS WITH CRASH COURSES
- Saturation

WHAT MAKES THE IDEAL TEAM?

SUMMARY
- Optimum duration • Conclusion

WHY A CRASH COURSE?

'I would like to book a week's crash course in Russian. I am a complete beginner. I cannot attend weekly classes and open/distance learning courses are not practical either. The only possible solution is to have a week away from the office and concentrate totally in that time on learning Russian.'

'I have been studying German on a two-hour-a-week basis for two years. I am going to Germany on a business trip and I would like to have a week's crash course prior to my journey.'

'I have been offered a job with a French company on the condition that I can speak French. Twenty years ago I studied French to 'O' level at school. How long will it take me to speak French well?'

For these and many other reasons, people decide to undertake a crash course in a foreign language. On some occasions the crash course will form part of a carefully planned strategy, but on others it is a last or desperate resort to learn to speak a language in a short time.

Whatever the initial reasons, those about to embark on a crash course should be aware of the many factors which can either make the experience successful and worth the investment, or achieve only a mediocre result (which sometimes may be made to *appear* good) and hence not worth the investment of time, effort and money on the part of the student.

Advantages and disadvantages

First of all, there are two basic types of crash course available, *residential* (8.30 am–10.00 pm) and *non-residential* (9.00 am–5.00 pm) – each has relative advantages and disadvantages (see table opposite).

When comparing residential with non-residential courses, we find that the results achieved on residential courses are much better than on non-residential ones. However all the advantages and disadvantages are based on the assumption that the tutoring and general course facilities are of a good and equal standard in all situations. Unfortunately, in reality, the standard of tutoring varies greatly from supplier to supplier and even within the same training company it can also vary considerably, depending on the skills of the individual tutors.

Most students understandably dread the thought of finding themselves immersed in an intensive residential course (8.30 am–10.00 pm) in the hands of poorly skilled tutors.

Type	Advantages	Disadvantages
Residential		
• in UK	• lower cost • easier to visit and assess/evaluate	• other than when talking to tutors the student will always speak in English
• abroad	• student immersed in a real situation and so speaks in the target language all the time	• higher cost • longer journey may add to demands on student
Non-residential		
• in UK	• lower cost • on call in case of emergencies at work or home	• student is still part of an English-speaking environment • during the course there may be interference from work and/or personal life • switching from target language to English and back is not as effective
• abroad	• student immersed in a real situation • speaks in the target language all the time* • concentration better because student is out of daily routine	• higher cost

* This is how it should be! In most cases, though, the student tends to find himself with another English speaker in his free time.

CAN YOU MEASURE STANDARDS AND QUALITY?

The standards and quality of courses can vary considerably and are difficult to measure. One rule of thumb is to look for quality of *preparation*, efficiency of the *organisation* itself, how well they convert promise into *practice* and, of course, the *results*.

Starting with the most important first, we can compare *results* achieved by different people attending different courses on a one-to-one teaching basis, but these results would be valid only if the people involved possessed the *same learning ability*, the *same motivation* and were studying the same language and started the courses at the same level and so on. In other words, in the case of two or more students in a group, the greater number of factors involved, the more difficult it is to compare results between people.

Reducing the risk of poor results

Nevertheless, there are ways of reducing the risk of poor results; when choosing a supplier:

- visit the establishment first before contracting the supplier;
- inform the supplier of your long-term objectives;
- establish clearly the programme that you will follow;
- speak to students who are finishing or have completed a crash course;
- ask to experience a sample hour or half-hour teaching session;
- find out how much you are expected to achieve by the end of the course; and
- find out how many tutors will be involved. (Ideally there should be two. Three would be a second best choice, but one alone, or more than three, would not be as effective.)

If you are considering providing a large contract you should also ask:

- what sort of training or staff development provision is in existence. (Look for evidence that one of the aims of the programme is the achievement of effective team performance.)

Those training centres or colleges which make a good impression should be tried, making sure as much as possible, that the students your company sends there are at a sufficiently similar level for you to be able to make the necessary comparisons at the end of the courses. Initially, you could send three learners of similar age/ability/motivation to three separate language schools for the same length of time in order to compare outcomes before your company draws up a long-term contract with any single provider.

SETTING REALISTIC OBJECTIVES

Before establishing objectives and developing a programme of study, a student must know clearly why he or she needs to learn a foreign language and in which situations the language will be used.

By discussing operational needs with an experienced language consultant or supplier, a language needs' schedule can be developed. Following that, and bearing in mind the student's availability to attend classes, ability to learn languages, and the time that is required to achieve the targets, an action plan can then be designed.

Case study 1: where it can go wrong

A company needed to send three engineers to a Spanish-speaking country. They informed the training manager that they were complete beginners and a week's crash course was booked.

The only information that the language centre received was that the students were complete beginners and that they needed to reach survival level very quickly.

The course started and almost immediately the tutor found out that two engineers were quite extroverted and highly confident at speaking Spanish, because they remembered a few words and expressions which they had picked up during holidays in Spain. The other engineer, who was also the oldest and slightly introvert, was a real beginner who didn't know a word of Spanish.

By the end of the first day, it was evident that were the three students to remain together two of them would not benefit from the course as much as they could and the third student would be so frustrated and upset that he would not learn anything.

The company was contacted and they agreed to split the group into two. By the end of the five days' crash course the first two students had reached an elementary survival level. The third student didn't overcome his earlier frustration and unfortunately became completely demoralised and ended the course speaking and understanding very little Spanish.

There should be objectives and targets for each component of the plan and, naturally, if this contains more than one crash course, for each of them.

A crash course, particularly if on a residential basis, may consist of up to 50 hours of organised learning distributed over five days. This is a considerable number of hours which should be reflected in the objectives and targets to be achieved by the end of the course.

Sometimes the expectations of a company or a student may be too unrealistic. Here is a possible guide:

- the supplier should carefully assess the student's language learning needs and ability, as well as his present level, before the course begins;
- the supplier, together with the student, should identify the course objectives and targets;
- after the first day of the course, the objectives and targets should be reviewed and if necessary changed; a further review should be undertaken on day three;
- at the end of the course there should be a full evaluation; if the objectives and targets have not been met, the reasons for that should be sought; and
- if the crash course forms part of a total learning plan, then it must be reviewed within the wider context.

Case study 2: where it can go right

A manager had two months notice to move to Calais where he would be working with French-speaking colleagues. His knowledge of French was very limited, based on what he could remember from two years of study at school many years ago. He could only give up five days leave to study.

He was interviewed at a language centre and advised to follow a two-week distance learning course, with tutor support, followed by a three-day residential crash course, three more weeks distance learning, finishing with a two-day residential crash course.

The targets for each stage had been identified and agreed with the student before the course, following a thorough initial assessment and needs analysis.

At the end of the full course the student had achieved a good enough basic working knowledge of French to enable him to undertake with confidence his duties in Calais.

Quite often a crash course forms only one part of a much longer language-learning plan. In such cases, it makes good sense to concentrate on only certain quite specific objectives and activities during the short course, e.g. on speaking and listening skills. Also, life-like simulations are possible and beneficial and provide necessary variation during intensive courses.

On some occasions it is necessary for specific company materials to be incorporated into the foreign language learning programme, e.g. brochures of specifications and other company literature. When this is the case, it is essential that the language tutors who design the learning programme be sent the actual material in plenty of time so that it can be studied and incorporated at the most appropriate point and in the most effective manner.

Otherwise, the course materials should, as far as possible, reflect life-like situations which the student may encounter. They should also be varied and motivating.

It should be obvious that crash courses can be a very effective and efficient way of achieving language targets. This is the case whether they are run independently or combined with other forms of delivery. However, the procedure and recommendations outlined above should be followed in order to ensure that the experience is as successful as possible.

PROBLEMS WITH CRASH COURSES

Assuming that the learning environment and materials are adequate, there are two main type of problems which may arise from a crash course:

- under-achievement due to mismatch of supplier and student expectations; and
- learner overload or saturation.

The first is likely to occur when students are sent on a crash course because the company has decided that they should learn to speak a particular language. The students arrive at the centre without a clear indication of the process which they are expected to go through. Their expectations are based on previous experiences at school and these are very different from those which have been prepared for them.

The problem of 'saturation' may be encountered when everything appears to be going extremely well. The students start the course learning well and fast; then suddenly they begin to make mistakes, using structures incorrectly which they thought they had already mastered. Everything becomes confused and the students start to feel exhausted and demoralised.

The first of these problems is a sign of poor preparation; either the system for selecting the best supplier has broken down, or the supplier has not briefed the student adequately on what progress can be made during the course.

The second problem can arise when one or more of the following happens:

- the tutor finds that the student is very able and introduces new material too fast;
- the tutor is unable to read the student's body-messages of 'Enough', or 'I am finding it too fast', which the student starts to

exhibit even before realising what is happening;
- the student and tutor leave the teaching room only for short and infrequent periods during the day;
- the student finds the pace of the course too slow, so pushes the teacher to go faster and 'crashes'; and/or
- the tutor does not make the learning steps sufficiently small to make the learning experience comfortable.

To understand the problem of saturation, imagine that there are two 'pools' in the brain – the 'pool' of understanding and the 'pool' of knowledge.

When a new structure or word is introduced and the students understand its meaning, they can begin to use that new structure/word correctly. After a while they may come to believe that they know it and will not forget it.

The tutor will continue to introduce other structures/words and so the process will be repeated again and again. Then suddenly, when the course appears to be going perfectly well, the problem of saturation arises.

Saturation

The process of learning can be visualised diagrammatically as in figure 1.

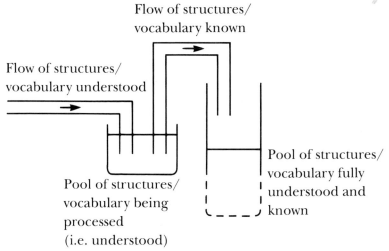

FIGURE 1: *The learning process*

Think of language learning as a two-stage process. Students understand new words and structures which the tutor introduces, but they still need to process them before they are fully understood and remembered. The intermediate stage is really the 'piping' of information from the short-term pool to the long-term storage vessel. Saturation can arise when too much new language is piped through and the intermediate pool overflows.

The task that even skilled tutors on crash courses in particular face is to regulate both flows concurrently, so that the learning process does not break down and the student does not become confused, demoralised and demotivated.

The diameter of the pipes through which the flow of structures/vocabulary runs will be determined by the student's ability at learning languages and other significant factors, already discussed in chapter 3.

Depending on how successful the learning process is, different types of learning can result; represented by graphs *a–d* (see figure 2).

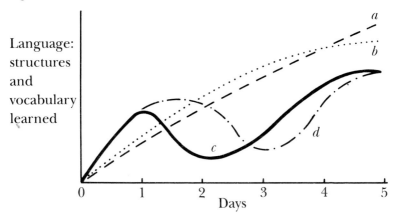

FIGURE 2: *Different types of learning*

Type 'a'

This is the ideal situation, when the team of tutors are able to control the flow of learning and use it in the most efficient way:

- the language is presented in steps sufficiently small to make the learning process comfortable and effective;
- the student is completely immersed in the target language during the duration of the course;

- the environment is appropriate and used effectively;
- there is good team work amongst the tutors involved; and
- the tutors are able to read the student's body language.

Type 'b'

Often this curve is presented as the ideal or most effective one. However, when observing the learning process we find that:

- the teaching steps could have been made smaller;
- the tutors spent much more time speaking than the student;
- the environment was not good or not used effectively; and
- saturation point is not far off.

Type 'c'

In this situation the flow of structures/words understood is so fast that the student has reached saturation point in one day. Although the student overcomes the saturation problem later on, the results of the course are not as good as they should have been. Time has been wasted and the student possibly demoralised.

Type 'd'

In this situation the flow of structures/words understood by the student may be as fast as in the previous case, but because the student has a greater ability to learn the particular language, the saturation point occurs later.

The results achieved at the end of the course should be better because the student possesses a greater ability for learning languages.

Generally, language tutors are trained to teach students in a conventional way, i.e. one/two/three two-hour sessions per week. If they have not undertaken the appropriate training to teach a language in a crash course format, they will not have the necessary skills and their work will not be very effective.

WHAT MAKES THE IDEAL TEAM?

There are some British and overseas tutors who are virtually bilingual, very much aware of the difficulties that the students may encounter when understanding particular structures and who are equally skilled as teachers. In these cases there are no practical differences between native and non-native tutors. Such tutors, however, are not often found and as a compromise the best team could consist of one native and one British speaker, who nevertheless are able to perform as a team and use their relative strengths and particular skills in the most effective and efficient way in the pursuit of student success.

But let us consider the arguments for and against native and non-native speaker tutors.

Type of tutor	Advantages	Disadvantages
• British tutor	• speaks the language of the student and can anticipate problems that he may encounter • has studied the foreign language himself and thus possesses a good understanding of its difficulties • when necessary can speak slowly, sympathise with the student's difficulties and take appropriate action.	• presents some inauthentic language • does not have the mannerisms or expressions of a native speaker, nor the background knowledge and experience of life in the target country.
• Native speaker	• speaks the language in a totally natural way (pronunciation, choice of vocabulary, structures, mannerisms) • authenticity is highly motivating to student.	• may speak too fast and present the language in an unnecessarily difficult way • may find it difficult to sympathise with student's difficulties. In some cases, may not speak the student's language.

SUMMARY

At the beginning of this chapter I suggested some reasons why students decide to book a crash course. If you are to make the right decision you need a clear understanding of the relative advantages and disadvantages of this method compared to the traditional one, two or three sessions per week format.

The advantages and disadvantages listed below assume that in all cases the tutors are equally skilled and that the courses are held in a suitable environment.

	Advantages	**Disadvantages**
• Crash courses	• no external distractions during learning process • very encouraging and motivating particularly for the complete beginner, as a result of the rapid progress made • quick way for intermediate/ advanced students to concentrate on and achieve specifically identified objectives • extremely effective immediately before going abroad • student uses the language learned in life-like situations.	• student loses his command of the language quite quickly without appropriate reinforcement • expensive in the short term • absence from work may be disruptive • may be stressful.
• Weekly classes	• student does not have to be absent from work • the pace of learning is more relaxed • student can retain the material covered for longer periods.	• it may take a long time for the student to achieve his objectives and make noticeable progress; this can be demoralising and demotivating • student not always

able to concentrate
fully due to work
pressures imposing
on his concentration
- often little or no
back-up work is
done between
classes, so
reinforcement of
new language hardly
happens.

A crash course can thus be the ideal format for learning in the following cases:

- as a booster or refresher course for an intermediate or advanced level student, before a visit to the country concerned, or before the arrival in the country of a potential client; and
- as a survival/'ice-breaker' package for a complete beginner student in similar situations to those noted above. In this case the course should take place immediately before the language is needed, otherwise the student may not be able to retain newly acquired linguistic skills. If this is not possible, arrangements must be made to practise and/or refresh these skills in the interim.

Besides the above occasions a crash course may form part of any overall company language learning strategy and can be used in combination with other forms of delivery so that the most effective results are achieved. For example:

- complete beginners who find out that they have to travel to a particular country soon should try to fit in a few hours of study before the crash course, either face-to-face with a tutor or on a distance learning package basis with the support of a tutor. Even if they only manage to study for some six hours, these will prove highly beneficial, provided that there is a link between the tutor involved in the pre-course package and the crash course tutors;
- a member of the sales division who finds it difficult to attend tuition on a regular weekly basis, may follow a line of study involving several short (e.g. three days) crash courses, which

could take place at appropriate intervals; some form of complementary study between crash course modules would also
prove beneficial; and

- a student following a series of classes on a regular basis, either
in-company or at a centre, would benefit from a crash course at
an appropriate time; the crash course would act as a morale
and motivation booster and could offer the student the opportunity to use the language learned in life-like situations.

Optimum duration

In each individual case there exists an optimum length for the
crash course. In most, five days prove to be very beneficial – the
student is not away from his work too long and it is easily possible
to achieve worthwhile, identifiable objectives.

For students who are being sent abroad for a period of a year
or more, and who are at a beginner level, two weeks, with a
weekend free, proves very appropriate and effective. In this
particular case it may be worthwhile for the wife or husband of
the student also to join the course, particularly for the first week
when general social language is introduced. The second week
could be dedicated to more work-related situations and technical
language.

Conclusion

The crash course has an important place amongst the range of
training options available. It has strengths and weaknesses,
however. It is particularly effective for business people who need
to make rapid progress in starting a new language or who are
short of time in the lead up to going abroad. As a stop-gap
measure, it is only of limited value outside the context of a
well-developed integrated training strategy.

CHAPTER SEVEN

COMPUTER-ASSISTED LANGUAGE LEARNING

GRAHAM DAVIES

CAN COMPUTERS REPLACE LANGUAGE TUTORS?
• Computers in a multi-media language centre

WHAT KIND OF COMPUTER?

CATEGORIES OF CALL PROGRAMS
• Vocabulary programs' • Verb conjugation programs' • Grammar programs' • Hypertext packages' • Correspondence training packages' • Authoring packages' • Audio-enhanced packages' • Interactive videodiscs

CONCLUSION

CAN COMPUTERS REPLACE LANGUAGE TUTORS?

An important consideration for the training manager is the extent to which it is possible to replace the language tutor with a computer. There are many myths surrounding computer-assisted language learning and, unfortunately, many charlatans around who are only too prepared to take advantage of British business executives' lack of knowledge of foreign languages and offer them instant solutions, aided and abetted by technology.

Imagine the following scenario:

> A business trainee is sitting at a computer following a language training program. Step-by-step, the computer presents the essential vocabulary and structures. These are accompanied, where appropriate, by still and animated graphic images, photographs and video recordings. As new words and phrases are introduced, authentic male and female voices pronounce them and the learner repeats them. The learner's voice is recorded by the computer and played back. Any errors in pronunciation are indicated graphically on screen. Offending syllables are highlighted and additional practice is offered on sounds which the learner finds difficult. At the end of each presentation sequence, the computer tests the learner's grasp of the new vocabulary and structures, marking and recording those words and phrases which have been imperfectly recalled and offering feedback on points of grammar that the learner appears to have misunderstood. The learner has access at all times to an on-line dictionary, a reference grammar and verb con-jugation tables. At the end of the work session the learner's progress is recorded by the computer, which enables the thread to be picked up at the next session. In addition, the learner's progress records – along with those of all the other trainees following the same course – can be accessed at any time by the training manager.

As yet, such a scenario exists only in the dreams of the training manager. There is no integrated software package that will do all the things detailed above. There are, however, a number of software packages that will do most of them independently – and many of these are described below. The onus is therefore still on the teacher or the learner to manage the learning process.

COMPUTERS IN A MULTI-MEDIA LANGUAGE CENTRE

It is worth reiterating the implied warning in the above scenario that technology alone is not the final solution to language training. A multi-media language centre that includes computers may, however, make a major contribution. This might consist of the following hardware – in order of priority:

- audiocassette recorders;
- videocassette recorders;
- a satellite TV installation; and
- computers.

Audiocassette recorders should be of the audio-active comparative (AAC) type, which allow the learner to listen, repeat, play back and compare his/her voice with the native speaker model. These are available at a modest cost from specialist suppliers such as Coomber.

The other items of equipment, videocassette recorders and a satellite TV installation, can be obtained from a wide variety of suppliers. It is important, however, that the satellite TV installation is set up to receive and record the foreign language broadcasts that will be most useful, e.g. news broadcasts and documentaries, which will prove invaluable to the intermediate and advanced learner as an authentic source. Here, it is difficult to give advice that will be valid for more than a few months, as satellite TV stations are constantly appearing and disappearing. Up-to-date information is contained in the monthly publication *Satellite TV Europe* (UK Satellite TV Europe, c/o Select Subscriptions Ltd, 5 Riverpark Estate, Berkhampstead HP4 1HD).

There are also purpose-built multi-media systems which combine all the above equipment. These can be obtained from suppliers, such as Tandberg, R. J. Education or Sony.

WHAT KIND OF COMPUTER?

One advantage of computer-assisted language learning (CALL) is that the essential hardware required to run many software packages is readily available on the desktops of large numbers of employees in a typical modern business. There is a wide variety of inexpensive CALL software packages that will run on the two commonest types of desktop computers in the business world: the

IBM PC or compatible, and the Apple Macintosh.

A standard IBM PC or compatible computer is ideal for CALL. 'Standard' in this context implies a 286 processor, 640K RAM, DOS 3.0 or higher, an EGA or VGA colour monitor, a 20-megabyte hard disk, and a single 3.5-inch or 5.25-inch floppy disk drive. Anything better or bigger than this is a bonus and not essential. A mouse is a useful extra.

Apple Macintoshes come in a variety of different guises these days, and this is not the place to discuss the whole range in detail. Most CALL software will run on the Mac Plus or higher. A hard disk is a must, but a colour monitor is not necessary. The minimum requirements are: 2 megabyte RAM, System 6.0 (or higher) and *Hypercard* software. A mouse comes as standard equipment on the Mac.

Specialised CALL software may require additional equipment, e.g. an audio card for voice output and recording, a CD-ROM drive or a videodisc player. This equipment is discussed in more detail in the relevant sections below.

CATEGORIES OF CALL PROGRAMS

Vocabulary programs

One of the simplest – and most traditional – types of CALL program is the vocabulary program. Such packages offer the learner lists of words and phrases, organised thematically into meaningful groups such as eating and drinking, travel, etc. The learner is presented with the English and foreign-language versions of the words and phrases and then tested on them. The test is a computerised version of the old-fashioned 'vocab test' that schoolchildren dread. The learner enters the answers at the keyboard and is given immediate feedback, with a mark at the end of the test and the opportunity to revise any wrong answers *ad infinitum*.

Although memorising lists of words does not automatically make a good linguist, no one has so far found an ideal way of fixing in the language learner's head the several hundred common words that are essential for basic survival situations. Vocabulary programs do seem to help, and knowing the meanings of a substantial number of words builds up confidence in the beginner. But the learner must be provided with additional practice in using the vocabulary in meaningful contexts – which is where the teacher comes in.

Vocabulary programs are cheap and cheerful, costing on average £20 to £40 per language, and offering about 2000 basic words and phrases. Typical examples of packages of this type are *The French Mistress, The German Master, The Spanish Tutor* and *The Italian Tutor*. All are produced and published by Kosmos and run on IBM-compatibles.

A more elaborate series of vocabulary programs is produced and published by Gessler, New York. These are entitled: *La bataille de mots* (French), *Wortgefecht* (German), *La batalla de palabras* (Spanish). An important feature of this series is that the words appear both in lists and in meaningful contexts. There is also a 'battle of words' game in each package. The programs run on IBM-compatibles.

Both the Kosmos and the Gessler series allow the language teacher to set up new lists of words.

A ready-made vocabulary series designed specifically for the business learner is published by Topware. The vocabulary is divided up into four sets entitled: *The Businessman, The Operator, The Secretary* and *The Traveller*. Each set is available in French, German, Spanish and Italian, at about £50 per set.

Verb conjugation programs

A second traditional type of program presents and offers practice in the conjugations of irregular verbs. The main feature verb conjugation programs have in common with the previous category is the decontextualised test. Two typical programs in this category – which their author describes as 'unashamedly old-fashioned' – are Locheesoft's *German Verbs* and *French Verbs* packages. Both enable the language learner to look up the conjugations of irregular verbs and then to undergo a test on a chosen range of verb and tense types.

Knowing the conjugations of irregular verbs will not automatically transform the learner into a good communicator, but failure to use the right form of a verb can cause a breakdown in communication under certain circumstances. It is possible to justify this type of program on the same grounds as stated above with regard to vocabulary packages, but the warning must be issued that additional contextualised practice – preferably with a teacher – is vital.

Grammar programs

This is the last of the trio of categories of traditional programs that reflect the approach to language learning with which the older learner is probably familiar. This sounds like a criticism but is not intended as such. Language acquisition is a complex and often misunderstood process, and language teaching methodologies are rather like fashions in clothing. There is now a strong indication that grammar – like the miniskirt – is making a comeback. In any case, adult learners often feel more secure in the comfortable world of vocab, verbs and grammar – areas which they can easily identify and where they feel they can measure their progress. And it can be argued that, if the computer can take care of the nuts and bolts of a language, the teacher then has more time to concentrate on communicative skills.

There are relatively few complete grammar tutorial and practice programs. One of the best-known packages is *CLEF*. It was originally produced for adult beginners in Canada, and aims to guide the adult learner through the labyrinth of basic French grammar. It consists of 62 lessons, beginning with *le*, *la* and *les* and ending with uses of the subjunctive and passive. Each lesson follows the same pattern, beginning with an optional tutorial on a point of grammar, followed by a review of the new vocabulary in the lesson and finishing with a series of contextualised exercises. *CLEF* is remarkable for the discreet feedback and help it offers the learner. *CLEF* is available in the UK from Camsoft.

TUCO is a German grammar package, produced by Ohio State University. It is not as comprehensive as *CLEF* and lacks the tutorial element, but it does offer useful exercises and sensible feedback. *TUCO* is available in the UK through Camsoft.

Un menu français is another package in this category that

deserves a mention. It was originally produced in Denmark and offers a large number of exercises on basic French grammar, all with discreet feedback. There is also an on-line reference grammar, a dictionary and an editing facility for teachers who wish to amend or add to the main body of material. *Un menu français* is available in the UK from Camsoft.

Hypertext packages

Hypertext is a relatively new concept in CALL and it is difficult to do this exciting new medium justice simply by describing it. Let us suppose you wish to study a language through a very traditional medium: a book. You normally start at Lesson 1 and work your way towards the end. Occasionally you turn to the back to look up vocabulary or points of grammar, but your progress follows a fairly straight path. This is, however, a very inefficient method of learning, as knowledge of any subject is rarely acquired in such a linear way. By the time you have reached Lesson 5 you have forgotten most of the vocabulary and grammar in Lesson 1. In addition, it is also difficult for you to explore the path ahead if you have a burning desire to follow up a particular point in more detail.

In a hypertext environment the information presented to you and the exercises designed to test your knowledge are stored in the form of discrete *frames*. Together, the frames form a *stack*. You may begin by reading the first frame, but from this point on you can *navigate* your way through any of the other frames in the stack, in any order. As you read a text frame you realise you need more information on certain words and structures. So you use the computer's mouse to point at an unknown word, which happens to be a verb. You click the mouse button and the verb is translated. Now you are curious about the verb's form, so you point at a *conjugation* box and click. This reveals a table of conjugations of the verb. Now you want to know about the usage of the verb, so you point at and click on a *usage* box, which reveals examples of the verb in different contexts. So you now have three frames, stacked one above the other. Clicking the mouse on a series of *backtrack* boxes brings you back to the original text you were reading.

One of the most accessible series of hypertext packages for IBM-compatibles is known as *Traveller's Guild*. There are French, German, Spanish and Japanese packages in the series, offering a substantial collection of texts and exercises for the business traveller. They are not expensive at around £80 apiece, and are available from Guildsoft.

Guildsoft also markets a series of similar packages for the Apple Macintosh known as *Hyperglot*. These are much more sophisticated and include digitised sound recordings of native speakers that can be played back on a standard Mac. The range of languages is wider and includes French, German, Spanish, Italian, Russian, Chinese and Japanese. All the packages run in conjunction with the Mac's own *Hypercard* package.

Correspondence training packages

This is a rather specialised category of software that is aimed directly at the business user. Packages in this category can be used both as training aids and as tools for the speedy generation of business letters in foreign languages. The two best-known packages of this sort are Multi Lingua's *LinguaWrite* and Primrose Publishing's *Tick-Tack*.

Both packages consist of a set of multi-lingual glossaries of standard business correspondence phrases. In *LinguaWrite* you search for a keyword, e.g. *offer*, and the computer displays a variety of phrases containing it. You select the one you want, e.g. 'we can offer an introductory discount of ... %', and the phrase will automatically be translated into French, German, Spanish or Italian. A skeleton letter can be built up in this way and finally tidied up in a word-processor of the user's choice. Any amendments can be checked with a foreign language spelling checker, which can be supplied for most leading word-processors, e.g. *Word Perfect* and *Microsoft Word*. *LinguaWrite* includes a *Builder* program which enables the user to add new words and phrases to the standard lists.

In *Tick-Tack* the principle is the same, but the package is also accompanied by its own word-processor, and it is necessary first to look up the required phrase in a handbook. The handbook gives you a phrase reference number, which you key in and then the corresponding phrase in the required target language is inserted on screen.

The more advanced language learner, who needs special practice in business correspondence vocabulary, benefits most from the use of these packages. A further enhancement might be an on-line dictionary, phrase translator and reference grammar, such as *The Language Assistant* – available in French, German, Spanish and Italian and obtainable through Camsoft in the UK.

Authoring packages

This category of programs is only of interest to the business trainer who has access to a teacher. This is because such programs are only empty shells that offer the framework for setting up a particular type of test or exercise. A teacher is therefore necessary to create material that ties in with a particular business's needs – which may of course be very useful if the business has to train its employees in very specialised areas of language and terminology. If the business has an on-site language teacher then such packages might be the answer. Alternatively, a local college or polytechnic could be commissioned to produce a set of tailor-made materials with selected authoring packages.

Wida Software's *Gapmaster* or Camsoft's *Gapkit* are authoring packages designed for producing gap-filling exercises, and Wida's *Choicemaster* is excellent for producing multiple-choice tests. There is also a very useful multi-purpose authoring package known as *Questionmaster*, which now offers the facility of sound without the need for an audio card.

There is a special category of authoring packages, in which the computer blanks out or mutilates the whole or the part of a text which the learner then has to reconstruct. These 'text reconstruction packages' have proved very popular in schools and colleges as back-up material linked to existing courses. Camsoft's *Fun with Texts*, and Wida Software's *Storyboard* and *Pinpoint* are typical examples, but there is as yet no body of business texts to accompany them.

Audio-enhanced packages

Programs with sound have already been briefly touched upon in the section on Hypertext packages. Up until recently, sound could not be taken for granted in CALL programs. Nowadays the choice is increasing.

The *Hyperglot* series (see above) includes a number of programs that make use of the inbuilt sound reproduction facility of the Apple Mac. If you connect a CD-ROM drive to your Mac, you have access to more substantial quantities of sound recordings. A CD-ROM drive is an additional expense, but it offers more flexibility. The compact discs that you run on such a device look like standard audio compact discs but, thanks to computer technology, they have enormous flexibility as mass storage media, and can be used not only to store sound but also text and pictures – including moving pictures. Because of the multiple purposes to which CDs of this type may be put, they are known as 'multimedia'.

An excellent example of a CALL CD-ROM package is *Hanzi*, which aims to teach over the written and spoken forms of about 2000 basic Chinese characters. It is a bargain at only $100 and obtainable from Dartmouth College, USA.

The *Traveller's Guild* series for IBM-compatibles (see above under 'Hypertext packages') can also be enhanced by the addition of a CD-ROM drive, but a speech output device (obtainable from Guildsoft) also has to be plugged into the back of the computer.

A number of audio enhancements for IBM-compatibles are now being marketed by Tandberg Educational Ltd. These include *Voicecard*, which is inserted into your PC in order to enable sound to be output and recorded. Tandberg also markets *Voicecart*, which is a package for creating your own audio-enhanced exercises. A complete French language package, known simply as *Paris*, which runs on a CD-ROM drive and makes use of *Voicecard 1000*, is also being marketed by Tandberg.

Interactive videodiscs

Finally, we come to the most sophisticated category of CALL software: interactive videodisc packages. These come closest to the dream – or nightmare – scenario described at the beginning of this chapter. They offer full-colour moving images, authentic sound and access to on-line help.

Expodisc Spanish was one of the first commercial CALL video-discs to be produced in the UK. It casts the learner in the role of assistant to the export marketing manager of a firm that wishes to sell its new product to Spain and Latin America. The assistant's task is to help the manager, the formidable Alison Robinson, plan the trip and survive in a Spanish-speaking environment. The language learner has access at all times to background help on Spain and Spanish customs, and an export database. Assistance on specific aspects of vocabulary, grammar and usage is always at hand, and subtitles in English and Spanish can be switched on and off at will. Further details are available from The Language Centre, South Bank Polytechnic.

The more recent *Connections* series, which is produced by Vektor Advanced Learning Systems and includes *Die deutsche Verbindung*, *La connection française*, is also aimed at the business user. This series includes a sound recording facility, whereby the learner can compare his/her voice with the native speaker model. The *Connections* series is marketed by Tandberg.

Although interactive videodiscs offer the most opportunities for teacher-independent learning, there is a price to pay: special-ised hardware and add-ons costing an extra £2000–2500 per computer, and a price-tag of around £2000 for each videodisc and the software accompanying it. The user needs an IBM-compatible with a special monitor, a Philips-compatible laserdisc player, a video overlay card and, for the *Connections* series, an audio card.

CONCLUSION

The categories of CALL software described above were deliber-ately set out in order of increasing complexity. The simplest vocabulary packages run on a desktop computer, more or less without any need for support from a teacher or technician. Authoring packages, however, demand an enormous input from the teacher's side, and on-site technical support is a *sine qua non* if the business trainer is considering setting up a multi-media language lab, especially if this is to include computers with sound facilities and CD-ROM drives and videodisc players.

Technology-based language training does not come cheap, but in the longer term it may offer an enormous saving. The key to progress in learning a language is *practice*. Obviously, being in the country where the language is spoken is the best form of practice, but the computer has one advantage over the teacher: it will offer the learner endless opportunities for practising listening, reading and responding to stimuli. It offers immediate feedback, allows the learner to go off at tangents and never tires.

There is no doubt now that CALL has come of age. In a business environment it must be a serious consideration.

CHAPTER EIGHT

SELECTING LANGUAGE TRAINING MATERIALS

ANNE STEVENS AND DOUG EMBLETON

THERE IS NO SINGLE ANSWER
• 'Which is the best course for me?' • There really is no single answer! • Who uses the materials?

DECIDING WHAT IS USEFUL
• What do language training materials cover? • Checklist of material types • How much will I learn? • What is available?

MYTHS AND FACTS
• 'Business-specific' materials? • Reality *v* advertising

THERE IS NO SINGLE ANSWER

'Which is the best course for me?'

'Which would be the best course for . . . ?' is a very common – and very understandable – question raised by almost every would-be, adult language learner. The aim of this chapter is to demonstrate that both the answer to this question and also the person providing the answer need to be *qualified*.

The answer itself has to be qualified because there is no simple equation which instantly matches course *x* with learning requirement *y*. Of course, this qualified response can come either as a great surprise or as a huge disappointment to many aspiring adult learners. 'Surely,' they would argue, 'if we are talking about a practical issue such as languages for business, shouldn't there be a pragmatic, business-like response?'

There are sound reasons why this is not the case, which is precisely why it takes a *qualified person* to provide you with the correct, measured response. After all, if it were simply a case of matching a specific requirement with a specific set of course materials then your local booksellers could display the same set of purchasing guidelines which are so common these days when selecting the right wine for the right food at the supermarket.

On this basis, a guideline such as 'this wine is a superb accompaniment to fish courses' would equate with 'this language course is ideal for chemical engineers operating in French-speaking countries'.

As we shall see in this chapter there is a need to:

- distinguish *types* of language training materials;
- be very wary of 'panacea' solutions and over-enthusiastic advertising;
- define whether you are acquiring language training materials as an individual (that is, for your own self-tuition) or whether you are acquiring materials for your organisation;
- be very clear about the definitions of courses as 'business-specific';
- be very clear that even when you have selected the right materials, the actual language learning process requires a great deal of effort; and, above all
- fully appreciate why there is no single answer.

There really is no single answer!

The previous comparison with the purchase of wine can be taken a few stages further in order to clarify some of the main reasons for the lack of a single, clinical answer to the question 'Which is the best course for . . . ?'. We can approach this in several stages of logical thought.

- There are many wines which are compatible with fish courses.

However, we generally talk about a *type* of wine when discussing such topics. Reference to a specific vineyard or trade name normally constitutes a recommendation. In the same way, this chapter will deal with *types* of language training materials. Within these types there will be specific courses which suit your individual palate more than others. For example, you may be the sort of person who responds best to structured, grammar-based development of ideas within a course. You may have an ear which prefers studio-recorded audio cassettes to realistic, 'live' recordings. You may be so computer-literate that the use of computer-assisted language learning (CALL) is right up your street for consolidation work. These and other factors are very significant.

- Coming back to our comparison with the purchase of wine, we can also say that a language *per se* constitutes the whole meal and not simply one of the courses or dishes within the meal! A well-balanced menu will include various hues and flavours of wine and, perhaps, an aperitif and a liqueur.

Certainly, all good teachers of foreign languages to adults will use a whole mixture of materials and approaches.

- When obtaining wine we may well either take a chance or rely on the supermarket guides in the context of our own self-catering. On the other hand, if we are dining out we might normally take the advice of the wine waiter. However, even the wine waiter will offer you a *choice* of wines at a range of prices, all of which will 'do the job'.

If we apply this logic to the selection of language training materials we can now begin to appreciate that:

- the choice also depends on what sort of meal you want and what you want to pay (both in terms of money and in terms of *your time and commitment*);
- it is inappropriate to refer to specific, 'named' training materials; and
- a good meal – and a good language training outcome – are ideally made up of several types of courses.

Therefore, if you simply wish to acquire a little 'survival language', the language training material equivalent of fast food will do. On the other hand, if you wish to really make progress and handle fairly complex situations, you should be prepared to look at the whole menu and choose the best combination for the full meal. You must also be prepared to foot the bill for this option in terms of the time and commitment which you will devote to learning.

Who uses the materials?

A clear distinction has to be made between:

- purchasing materials as an individual for self-tuition;
- purchasing materials on behalf of your company or organisation (e.g. for the training centre); and
- using courses under the guidance of a tutor and skilled language trainer.

The best general guideline is that if your needs come within the first category you should carefully read the guidelines both in this chapter and in chapter 5 ('Self-tuition'); if they come within the second category, you should still read the guidelines in this chapter but also seek expert advice from a language consultant; if they come within the third category, you should already be on the receiving end of expert advice – but this chapter will help you to assess how good that advice really is!

Certainly, anybody in the third category should be experiencing the end result of the professional linguist's disinclination to name one course for one requirement. Their tutor should be using a range of materials. There will probably be a coursebook which the group is following as the 'core' material, but the tutor will also be using the 'best' parts from other courses, authentic materials, materials developed personally by the tutor, and so on. There is no definitive course in any language which answers each and every need.

For this reason, any request for a definitive, commercially available course for a given requirement is not denied by the expert linguist simply because it is difficult. It is also denied because it is inappropriate. Whether you are seeking advice for self-tuition purposes or for in-company objectives the message is clear – first of all, you must know about different *types* of courses, just as you would need to know about types of wine. The choice of the specific material may then boil down to a selection from a range of trade names and prices. On this basis, the expert will provide good advice based on his or her knowledge of the range of materials available and will, in collaboration with you, present a recommended package.

DECIDING WHAT IS USEFUL

What do language training materials cover?

As has already been pointed out, the selection of materials can mean many different things. It can vary from choosing a phrasebook at the airport to deciding upon the most appropriate coursebook and support materials for a company language training programme.

The phrasebook may need to do no more than assist you in moving around between engagements and possibly enable you to invite your colleagues for a drink in their own language. A quick perusal of the contents page should tell you whether it is appropriate for you or not and a look at the text should tell you whether the general presentation and layout suit your needs.

Selecting materials for self-tuition will require a very clear focus on your realistic objectives and your commitment. You may only wish to reach 'survival' level. If so, that's fine. The worst scenario occurs where there is a total mismatch between your own expectations of the outcome and the wilder and more exaggerated claims of some courses. This mismatch is enough to deter many people from even trying to learn a language a second time.

The choice of materials for training programmes is an altogether different matter, involving many important considerations. Other chapters refer to various preparatory stages and key decisions that have been made before the point of selecting the materials. Professional requirements now have to be matched to materials. It is highly unlikely that any one pack or package will contain all you require.

The materials that you find in bookshops or in catalogues all claim to have been designed to meet specific markets. They are also targeted at the major areas of need. However, it is not always easy to discover exactly what these are from the fliers and course descriptions and you may need to take a careful look before deciding whether this is really what you need.

You will quickly discover too that the greatest variety of materials exists for the major languages and that if your needs lie outside these, your choice is severely restricted. If, however, what you need in the way of materials falls within an area of considerable demand, you will be in the happy position of being able to select from among a variety of possible options. If, on the other hand, your needs coincide with only some, or just a few, of the target areas of the materials, materials selection will be considerably more complicated.

Checklist of material types

Language materials, whether a single textbook or an integrated package, can be characterised according to a number of different considerations:

- the type of course:
  - 'survival';
  - general;
  - business;
  - travel/tourism; or
  - sector-specific or business-specific;
- the title of course gives a general guideline as to what is covered:
  - phrasebook/traveller's guide;
  - short course;
  - refresher course;
  - study pack; or
  - longer course;
- where the learning is to take place:
  - classroom/group;
  - school/college/adult education;
  - individual tuition;

- self-study/assisted self-study; or
- open/distance learning; and
• the components of the package:
  - textbook;
  - textbook and workbook;
  - textbook with audio cassette;
  - video/broadcast material; and/or
  - software.

How much will I learn?

In reality, nobody can answer this question but you. The course description will tell you what is covered and – with total commitment and a lot of effort – this is what you will, in time, also cover. However, course descriptions are what they are. They are not a guarantee of your personal achievement. Above all, check that the book and materials are aimed at *adults*!

You will know from the contents whether the topics are of use to you. You may need to look in more detail to see whether the way they are treated suits you. Ensure that you have all the information you need.

Sometimes, course elements such as cassettes are supplied separately from books (a fact which may not be apparent when you pick up the coursebook, say, in this bookshop). In other courses, the packaging may not allow you to look through the contents and you may need to see a sample copy before making a decision.

One thing to bear in mind is that the claims of panacea solutions and promises of speaking the language fluently in a ridiculously short space of time should be treated with great circumspection. The back cover blurb and contents list will guide you on the coverage of the course or materials and you should look for some very clear and specific guidelines. After all, you may only want to 'survive' on a holiday or short business trip to another country. The courses which claim that this is their exact target – 'survival' – will be best for you. In any case, you will need all of the time claimed by the 'panacea' courses simply to reach 'survival' level. Above all, use your common sense! You probably don't make many other purchases on the basis of wild claims followed by exclamation marks.

What is available?

The materials can be a straightforward single book or an integrated course with different sorts of media. Sometimes the materials are packaged together, but where they are not, you may need to look at the details of the course to find out what is on offer.

Materials are made up of a number of component parts and they fall into a limited number of categories:

- textbook-based;
- textbook with workbook or worksheets;
- audio cassettes;
- video cassettes (see also chapter 9);
- software packages (see also chapter 7); and
- interactive video recordings (see also chapters 5 & 7).

Textbook-based

- These are few and far between these days as most have at least some accompanying audio material on cassette or CD. If, however, the book is the central feature of the learning material, then it is unlikely that the skill of speaking the language will be developed to any great degree. The textbook has the merit, however, of offering a structured approach to the language and many learners prefer this as it reinforces their own previous experiences of learning and they feel happy with it.
- A number of texts use imaginative extras to reinforce learning such as colours, pictures or sticky labels for the learner to post where they remind them of key points.

Textbook with separate workbook or worksheets

- This is a common combination these days. The presentation allows the new material to be quite separate from the more mundane practice of structures and language items.

- The use of a workbook or exercises with answers provided has the merit of giving instant feedback to the learner. The work completed may be used as a self-evaluation or self-correction procedure.
- If the learner is likely to carry out a lot of the work alone, this is an important feature in the design of the materials.

Audio cassettes

- Most language courses now integrate the use of audio material with their text. The quantity and quality vary enormously as do their usefulness. It is not practical to listen to and evaluate all such material in advance of the course, so specialist advice should be sought and also the experience of fellow learners.
- Material can be either recorded in a studio with a more or less scripted dialogue or interview for instance, or it can be based upon authentic recordings made 'live' in the country of the language and subsequently edited. This may be recorded 'live' or off-air as in a radio broadcast for example.
- Tutors and publishers have differing views of whether to use 'real-life' dialogue or scripted material on audio cassettes. The type of recording has important implications for the learner. Studio-recorded material provides a more 'comfortable' setting in that the language tends to be more clearly enunciated, and generally spoken more slowly. Live recording on the other hand exposes the learner to the 'real' language as it will be encountered in the country.

The pros and cons of studio and live recordings are:

Studio recordings	**Live recordings**
Advantages	*Advantages*
• Strictly controlled content	• 'Real' language used
• Delivery paced more slowly	• Uses varying registers
• 'Clean' recording	• Used under varying conditions
• Learner friendly	• Learner has to cope with reality
Disadvantages	*Disadvantages*
• Less realistic exposure	• Content less predictable

- Learner dependent on paced delivery
- Variable pace of language
- Language used under ideal conditions
- Less clarity of recording
- Learner less challenged
- More learner resistance

You may need to enlist some help from a language consultant to judge how useful the audio material is for you.

The quality, structure and clarity of the recording contributes considerably towards the difficulty or otherwise of the course. Elements within the recordings such as learner involvement, tone of voice, use of prompts and general encouragement are major factors.

The cassettes can also provide different ways of learning through exercises and practice which actively involve the learner in speaking and listening to the language. The exercises can be carefully designed to concentrate on particular aspects. Many learners find the use of cassettes stimulating and unobtrusive as they are mainly used in private, and for that same reason unthreatening. It is worth checking the course description to establish whether the tapes are designed for use whilst driving the car, for example. This process is very difficult if the course requires you to make constant reference to the book whilst using the cassettes.

Video cassettes

The benefits of video and broadcast material are covered in chapter 9. You will not find many courses offering 'off-the-shelf' video material. Those few which are available tend to be in the major European languages.

The video is used in a number of different ways:

- to simulate real situations;
- to record real activities;
- to exemplify teaching points; and
- to add a dimension to material presented elsewhere.

The advantages and disadvantages of the various types of recording are similar to those set out for audio. Video is ideal for illustrating non-verbal communication such as gestures. This is very useful and reassuring no matter what your level of proficiency.

For in-company language training where there is no video integrated into the course, and where it would be useful to have some visual element, it may be possible to introduce authentic material from elsewhere. One possibility is the use of training videos developed abroad to teach particular business skills. An exchange of such films could provide useful sources of linguistic and cultural information. Alternatively, it may be possible to commission the production of some video material specific to your needs.

Computer-assisted language learning (CALL)

CALL is used less frequently than video in business language training. The development costs are currently very high and the general usefulness of available materials is often not considered to be worth the investment. That said, it is a rapidly developing field and within a short time the use of CALL should make access to cheap and efficient language learning systems very much easier. This is covered in greater depth in chapter 7.

Interactive video (IV)

Interactive video is a very flexible medium and allows the learner to take an active part in the screened activity and offers the freedom to choose the nature of that involvement. Its main disadvantage is cost. Developing an IV pack is hugely expensive. As a result there is not too much available currently and what there is is of varying quality. This system has excellent potential for self-study or as a company resource for topping up existing or under-used skills. (See also chapters 5 & 7.)

As you can see, the range of materials ranges from the inexpensive to the expensive, from the basic to the sophisticated. There is no doubt that as time goes on, the hi-tech options will become increasingly important. For the moment, however, it is likely that a student who wishes to purchase materials predominantly for self-tuition will focus upon textbooks and audio/video cassettes, whilst in-company training schemes or universities and polytechnics will be the major users of CALL and interactive video.

MYTHS AND FACTS

'Business-specific' materials?

Terms such as 'business-specific' and 'vocational' are increasingly used in the context of language training materials. Indeed, there is a danger of their being over-used in the clamour on the part of the provider side of the equation to be seen to be responding to the needs of the 'business' side of the equation under the ageing banner of '1992 and all that'.

Whilst there certainly are some excellent business-specific or vocational language training materials available the following points should be remembered:

- the crucial factor is whether or not the materials have been developed for adults; and
- all of the research conducted within ICI Chemicals and Polymers Ltd (over many years) into the end uses of language skills confirms that:
  - the basic structures and building blocks are regarded as essential;
  - without these, anything 'business-specific' is simply a list of technical words;
  - anything 'business-specific' *in its entirety* is crushingly boring and limited since language is essentially about communication and communication, in turn, is about people; and
  - 'business-specific' terms can easily be added by individuals to sound and confident language skills. The same does not apply in reverse.

  For example, the phrases 'I would like you to reconsider the delivery date', 'I expect to arrive for the sales meeting at 3 pm', and 'I need to check the specifications' all contain more vocabulary of a general nature than they contain 'business-specific' vocabulary. However, a knowledge of the terms *delivery date*, *sales meeting* and *specifications* would be rendered all but superfluous without the ability to use the other 'general' words which support them.

Yes, you should certainly look for courses aimed at adults and, if you wish, for courses with a business content, or bias. However, do not start to believe that anything sold to you as *totally* 'business-specific' is necessarily relevant or practicable. The best language training materials specifically aimed at the business world manage to achieve a good balance between business-specific and general.

Reality v *advertising*

As we have seen in earlier chapters, one of the major deterrents to successful language training outcomes is the clearly lasting effect of unrealistic advertising claims. The problem is that such advertising is effective. People who do not achieve the desired – or advertised – outcome may blame themselves and assume that there is some magic quality – that they lack – which enables some people to learn languages more easily than others.

This is all a great pity because if only this powerful advertising could be harnessed to show people that learning a language can be fun, can be achieved by a variety of methods – at best, by a combination of these – but is genuinely hard work, then fewer people would give up at an early stage.

Whichever materials you select, do make sure that:

- you have established what you need to learn and why;
- if in doubt, you have consulted a language expert;
- the course appeals to you in its presentation (the course itself – not the advertising!);
- the course covers the right ground;
- the method suits you; and, above all,
- your objectives are realistic enough to be achieved.

CHAPTER NINE

TV/VIDEO
A User-friendly Guide

TERRY DOYLE

WHY TV/VIDEO?

• TV/video: what difference does it make? • Relevance to business • Advantages/disadvantages of TV/video

HOW DO TV AND VIDEO HELP LEARNING?

• TV/video: a practical guide • Using video effectively • Video strategies: a checklist • Self-tuition using video

LANGUAGE LEARNING MEDIA RESOURCES

• Criteria for selecting material

THE FUTURE OF TV/VIDEO

• Tourism or business? • Language learning from satellite • Interactive video

CONCLUSION

WHY TV/VIDEO?

There is perhaps an unnecessary mystique surrounding these media and their use in language learning. Some have made exaggerated claims, others have oversimplified their function to the point of banality. All the business learner really wants to know, though, is this: does it work?

Well, while we should not make exaggerated claims, neither should we underestimate the potential of TV/video when it comes to their place within an effective corporate language training strategy. Television in the broadcast mode is a powerful and persuasive instrument, and video in the hands of a prepared professional trainer or in a well-organised open learning environment is a rich and diverse tool for teaching and learning.

> 'I'd never have believed that following one beginners' course could improve my French so much – I am, quite frankly, astonished at the difference . . . and, you know, it has done wonders for my business relations too.' (Adult learner quoted in *Learning Languages from the BBC*, 1980)

The kind of testimonial that programme makers and course designers – as well as sales departments – pray for! But of course television and video are no more the instant panacea or miracle method than any other single means of learning a language. At their simplest they are both merely technical means of distributing messages, the one beamed directly into your living room or office, the other plugged into via the VHS machine. But in this case the medium is not the whole message.

TV/video: what difference does it make?

Part of the mystique surrounding TV/video is perhaps the confusion about the difference between them. We have already seen that, at one level, they are both simply different means of distribution. But there's more to it than that, and there are advantages and disadvantages to both. The important question is this: what can TV/video bring to your language training that no other medium can?

It's a truism to say that television motivates. A successful television series can attract hundreds of thousands, even millions of people to the notion of learning a language. It can persuade people of the learnability of the language and the accessibility of both the language and the culture. It conveys the simple message: here is an interesting culture, and learning the language (or even a bit of it) is the key to unlocking this culture. And, what's more, it brings language learning into everyone's living room, and within everyone's capability.

But motivation is only one function of television. Its real impact is both more subtle and more complex. In our monoglot culture the national media do not contain as a matter of course regular, essential, natural polyglot messages within the fabric of daily viewing or listening. In Sweden, Belgium, the Netherlands, Germany or Switzerland, readers, listeners and viewers are accustomed to a daily diet of information and entertainment in more than one language. Theirs is a multilingual media environment. The national consciousness of such countries is imbued with the notion that the existence of many languages is the norm, and language skills are consequently taken for granted. In our culture the norm is one language: English. When it comes to exposure to foreign languages, we are media-isolates.

The strength of broadcast television is that it can promote both foreign language awareness and the immediacy of other cultures to a mass audience, thereby opening a window on a wider world; while video can be used to develop further specific language skills and cultural insights. The diverse functions of each medium are equally crucial to trade and commerce.

Relevance to business

Perhaps the most important contribution television language programmes make to language learning is the initial shifting of attitudes, the broadening of perspectives, the altered perception of other languages, peoples and cultures. They add to the agenda of television as a whole and challenge the complacency of our resolutely monoglot culture.

> 'The coming of the Single Market combined with the re-drawing of frontiers in Eastern Europe mean that it is no longer a luxury to speak to foreigners in their own tongue – but a prerequisite.' (John Raisman, Deputy Chairman of British Telecom and Chairman of the Languages Lead Body)

By the very nature of the medium; television integrates language and culture. Whether through documentary film of daily life, interviews, observation, role-playing, dramatic dialogue, story-line, landscape or song, the presentation of language takes place inextricably intertwined with the culture of which the language is a part. It's a medium, therefore, which appeals and operates on many levels at the same time; a rich tapestry woven with all the professional skills and techniques brought to bear in the making of 'mainstream' television; a mine of authentic material showing language in action.

But of course you cannot 'learn' a language just by watching television, any more than you can learn to drive a car by watching car chases in cop shows. That's why these days the television programme is but the most visible element in a structured multi-media package, an integrated set of materials designed to develop different skills in different ways. The television programme should be of interest 'as television' even for those not interested in learning the language. High production values are

Advantages and disadvantages of TV/video

Using television

Advantages	Disadvantages
• cheap and freely available	• not always available when wanted
• attitude-changing	• transmission times inconvenient
• consciousness-raising	• uncontrollable pace
• motivation factor	• one-way communication
• structured, progressive, authentic material	• material may not be sufficiently business-specific
• professional production values	• cannot 'teach' by itself

Using video

Advantages	Disadvantages
• reasonably priced	• needs organising
• total control: limitless review	• equipment can cause problems
• self-pacing/more business-specific?	• needs servicing and maintenance
• two-way communication possible	• can waste time (trainer competence)
• lends itself to segmentation and chunking of material	• users and trainers may need training/induction

central to the process of motivation. Combined with other, complementary materials (radio, coursebooks, audio cassettes, work books, tutor's notes, transcripts, computer software), television can help true learning take place for those who choose to learn. And that's where video comes in.

Video may be an original product or it may just be broadcast television in another guise. The video cassette may contain a recording of the broadcast television programme, or it may be a version thereof – edited, re-edited, adapted, incorporating additional material perhaps, almost certainly with a guide on how to use the video. And this is where video scores over television: you can control it.

HOW DO TV AND VIDEO HELP LEARNING?

While television plants the idea that, for example, Japanese is (a) OK, (b) possible, (c) interesting, (d) fun, (e) useful and (f) possibly, profitable, video proceeds to capitalise on this idea by helping learners to develop both traditional language learning skills and strategies for communication.

Chapter 3 makes clear the link between the use of language learning strategies and successful performance in foreign language acquisition. Television and video programmes which promote language awareness and ways of approaching language learning are helpful tools in the learning process, especially at the beginning.

Many people prefer to be taught by a national of the country who brings the flavour and culture of the country into the classroom. It is also a prime role of television and video, whether or not you have access to native speakers, to bring to viewers and learners the look of the place and the people, a sense of the rhythm of daily life, examples of non-verbal behaviour, the sounds of natural speech at normal speed, music and song – all of which combine virtually to replicate the experience of 'being there'. This gives meaning, purpose and credibility to language learning.

TV/video can help language learners to:

- have fun while learning;
- develop listening comprehension (so-called 'receptive skills');
- in the video mode help develop speaking ('productive') skills;
- relate sound to picture to context and meaning: global learning;
- develop memory by association;
- learn by involvement;
- observe realistic language in action in meaningful situations;
- build vocabulary through repetition in a variety of contexts;
- think in the language without translation through English;
- reinforce meaning through subtitles where appropriate;
- involve the emotions to aid memory, e.g. through music and song; and
- perceive the transferability of basic structures from situation to situation.

TV/video: a practical guide

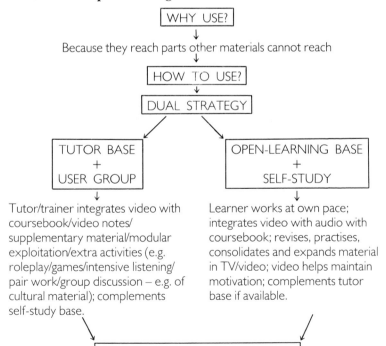

Using video effectively

In the hands of a good tutor one minute of television or video time can easily be expanded into 30 minutes or more of language teaching. The investment in video is, therefore, multiplied by a factor of some 30:1. Whereas the television programme will have told a complete story with its own continuous fabric, the video lends itself to a flexible variety of uses:

• the material can be presented in segments, sequences or modules;
• it can be shown with or without soundtrack;
• it can be viewed with or without subtitles;
• learners may summarise action/events after the sequence (past tense);
• learners may predict (re-using familiar language) action in advance (future tense);
• tutors can encourage guided listening;
• learners can develop gist comprehension or 'discrimination': picking out what they can understand, and using this to interpret surrounding incomprehensible material;
• personalised commentary can be improvised to picture;
• pair dialogues or role-plays can be based on situations in TV programme;
• tutor can encourage grammatical analysis and expansion of material 'skated over' in TV programme;
• tutor can use video to stimulate group discussion of cultural material in TV programme (in either English or target language);
• video segments can be used to introduce new topics or revise old ones; and
• use of video can grab and focus attention at the beginning of a session.

Television's use of involving dialogue, entertaining techniques (graphic devices, music, humour) and both aural and visual stimuli contributes to relaxation in learning. This has been shown to aid memory, vocabulary acquisition and pronunciation: you learn faster, speak better and with greater confidence if you are relaxed.

In the corporate context video can also be used to record role-play by students in the foreign language. Replays of edited highlights at the beginning of each session can provide added stimulus and almost certain amusement!

However, all of the above exploitation will only be effective if the tutor is in sympathy with the use of video, has been trained in its potential and comes to each video segment well prepared. It is important that the use of video in the class should have pace and rhythm. Sluggish use of the medium through inexperience, incompetence or ill-preparedness results in sluggish learning.

Video strategies: a checklist

Video is at its most effective when used as part of an integrated training programme in the hands of a good tutor. A good tutor/trainer should aim to:

- provide enough TV monitors to meet the demands of the number of learners on the course;
- allow for at least one back-up VCR;
- budget for hardware and software on a renewable basis;
- arrange for monitor/VCR maintenance;
- allocate space in a quiet room for independent video activity;
- allocate back-up technical facilities: audio/storage/print copying/time-shift recording and viewing (e.g. of broadcast and satellite material)/headphones for 'silent viewing' in the open learning mode;
- allocate time on a regular realistic basis for (a) self-tuition, (b) group work or (c) both; and
- allow for evaluation and feedback.

Self-tuition using video

In the open learning or self-tuition mode the organisation and management of time is essential to successful video-based language learning. One way of achieving this is to use the different components of a structured multi-media course to form a weekly framework of activities. These activities should be scheduled week-to-week over, say, a three to six month period on a diary basis. Make regular appointments with yourself, write them in your diary and treat them as you would an important business engagement. Here's one way to organise this appointment system:

Appointment 1:	watch TV programme/video	30 mins
Appointment 2:	work through corresponding unit (or part of unit) in coursebook; focus on understanding language	90 mins
Appointment 3:	listen to corresponding unit on audio cassette (several times)	60 mins
Appointment 4:	review coursebook material, including cultural sections; focus on practice of language in conjunction with audio cassette	90 mins
Appointment 5:	watch repeat of TV programme/ review on video	30 mins
	Total:	5 hours

At five hours a week it could take the average learner five months or so to reach the survival level of competence described in chapter 3, though some will progress faster than this. Total TV/video exposure time will be between five and eight hours (double if the review procedure recommended above is followed).

If you travel to work by car, or can combine incidental cassette use with another activity such as cooking, mowing the lawn, travelling by train or doing the washing-up, the regular appointments can be supplemented by constant review of audio material. However passive this exposure to the foreign language may be, the evidence is that the brain becomes increasingly attuned to the sounds of the language, aiding discrimination between words and patterns, and regular repetition helps vocabulary building, particularly when associated with visual recall of corresponding 'moments' in the TV or video programme.

If you use each element of a video-based learning package to structure your language learning in this way you'll find that your progress in assimilating and retaining new material and skills will be marked and encouraging – and the variety of exposure to different media will help sustain interest, reduce boredom and increase tolerance of the repetitiveness that is an inevitable feature of all language learning. It will also help you through periods where your learning curve reaches low-points, tempting you to drop out of language learning when progress wanes.

LANGUAGE LEARNING MEDIA RESOURCES

There is now a plethora of book/audio material on the adult language learning market, including a range of materials developed in association with TV and radio. These have often been innovative in methodology and content and may be used independently of the broadcasts themselves. Only recently, however, have they begun to take into account the particular requirements of the business learner.

Types of language learning pack

- *Travel pack with cassette.* This is the handy version of the self-tuition phrasebook and/or guide book, designed for the casual, or short-stay, holidaymaker or business traveller. It normally contains one audio-cassette for practising pronunciation of the set phrases in the book, which are largely touristic in content (e.g. ordering a meal, asking the way, saying 'goodbye', etc.). Although obviously not intended for the serious language learner, it can provide a few survival phrases without the complication of any grammatical explanation.
- *Self-tuition mini course with audio and/or video-cassettes.* With more detailed information on the language than the travel pack, this is a complete introductory course, though generally only intended for adults starting a language, or with very little knowledge to begin with. In academic terms, the course rarely takes the learner past O level/GCSE standard, but often goes beyond the 'survival' stage. The particular focus is on speaking and listening skills on everyday topics. There are usually a set of several cassettes, which are closely related to the units of the one or two coursebooks in the pack. A basic, even simplified,

form of grammar is introduced, as well as some terminology for business situations. Many of these packs are either linked to, or form part of, a radio and TV language and culture series. The more recent packs are accompanied by video-cassettes which illustrate life in the country itself and provide insights into the culture, which audio alone cannot achieve. The cost depends entirely on the number of cassettes and whether or not there is a video as well as an audio component.

- *Multi-media pack.* This is usually a fully comprehensive pack with various supplements designed for the serious language learner. It generally comes with a workbook, a range of in-built exercises, teacher's notes, video and/or audio cassettes, sometimes even software. These 'complete' courses are usually based on major TV or radio series. They are often available in open access language centres, and/or evening classes because the subject-matter they introduce can be complex and may need fuller explanation by a teacher. Generally, all four skills are developed, though the particular emphasis is still on verbal communication. More grammar is introduced than in the self-tuition courses. Although usually intended for beginners, they can progress through several stages of difficulty up to and including GCSE/O level, so they are sometimes used as the basic course material for a class of adults entering a public examination.

- *Training videos.* Versions of the multi-media and self-tuition videos above are sometimes packaged and re-designed for the business learner or company. They may be set partially or wholly in a business context and the supplementary materials are subordinate to the video, rather than the video supporting the coursebook. There are normally between five and eight hours of video material, three to eight hours of audio material, a coursebook, a teacher's book and a grammar/exercise workbook. They are intended for self-tuition at home or in an open learning centre, as well as for exploitation by language trainers. Some focus on specific needs, for example, using the telephone, but the majority of recent products concentrate on general business contexts, such as meetings, negotiations, visits, and so on. They can also be used as part of a face-to-face tuition course to illustrate business language in context.

Criteria for selecting material

As more language videos appear on the market, your company will need to be discriminating about what it buys. Here is a checklist of points to look out for:

- Check the language is relevant to your company's needs?
- Make sure it's up to date in both content and methodology.
- Make sure the content and design are relevant to your company's needs, and *adult* in conception and execution: courses designed for children will not prepare you and your staff for '1992' and beyond!
- Check that the production values meet the high expectations of today's sophisticated television viewer.
- Make sure the level and pace are right, and that the materials are flexible enough to be useful in both the tutor mode and the open learning mode for maximum cost-effectiveness.

THE FUTURE OF TV/VIDEO

Tourism or business?

Most people watching beginners' television language programmes do so for personal, travel or holiday reasons, rather than vocational or business purposes. Programme content has inevitably reflected this, though some series have attempted to do justice to the inherent value and interest of the society and culture in question as a whole rather than presenting them merely in a holiday context.

More and more, though, producers are devising programmes that appeal to the broadly defined 'visitor' (not just the tourist) in their linguistic and cultural content. There is an increasing perception of an audience which, in post-Single Market Europe, will be more mobile than ever before, with all that that implies for cross-linguistic and cross-cultural communication, and language programming is beginning to reflect this. This means of course that programme and course content is becoming more and more relevant to the visitor on business than before, which in turn means that TV and video-based courses are now a more appropriate and attractive language learning option for business people, with more business situations and 'business context' forming a natural part of course content.

Much existing audio and video material on the market, though perhaps not specifically or exclusively designed for business purposes, contains the kind of transactional and social language which is just as important for people travelling on business as more narrowly defined business vocabulary or etiquette. Since much business is in any case carried out in social or quasi-social situations and relationships such language will be just as essential. Courses on video which contain language and information on and about business practice and behaviour in the country of the language are of course worth special consideration.

The future in Europe will see a proliferation of structured video courses, at both beginners and more advanced levels; an explosion of foreign language television resource material; a growth in vocational and business-oriented syllabuses; more interactive video programmes; an increase in the production and marketing of TV/video-based multi-media packages designed for the corporate market, in an increasing variety of languages, from German, French, Spanish and Italian to Japanese, Korean, Arabic and the languages of Central and Eastern Europe.

As more vocationally qualified young people enter business and industry so will demand increase for the maintenance of language skills and cross-cultural competence begun at school. They will expect, even take for granted, the use of video as a training tool in the workplace (e.g. in conducting business simulations), since many of them will have come through courses which included the application of video alongside initiatives in electronic mail (Prestel, Télétel), direct satellite broadcast, audio-active-comparative cassette recording, telephone monitoring, word-processing and microcomputing, creating a strong link between language learning and information technology, and designed to meet the needs of business and industry.

Language learning from satellite

Broadcast television has from time to time provided series consisting of edited foreign television material in the original language, often backed up by verbatim transcripts and suggestions for follow-up in classes. Perhaps the most well-known of these was the long-running *Télé-Journal*, based on foreign language news bulletins, starting with France and eventually reaching as far as Mexico and the USSR.

But broadcast television cannot compete with satellite when it comes to the provision of such resources, since transmission slots are always scarce, even for structured series. Companies serious about the use of TV/video in language training should be equally serious about considering incorporating satellite television into their training strategy, since it is a rich, indeed inexhaustible source of real-life contextualised language material – as well as showing you what your counterpart is watching on television in Paris, Frankfurt, Milan or Madrid. The main problem is the one raised earlier – that of selection. This requires both expertise and time – to record, to organise and to exploit the material. And there is always the problem of copyright.

The innovative Olympus project is actively engaged in resolving such matters. Programming includes experiments ranging from how to learn Catalan for Spanish expatriates to live interactive tutoring of Japanese to Welsh schoolchildren, using on-screen light pens and telephone feedback. Video material may be backed up by printed support material accessed via personal computer.

Though no substitute for structured courses at the beginners' level, satellite resource provision has much to contribute, especially in the hands of an imaginative tutor, to the enrichment of language learning, particularly when it comes to developing the skills of understanding, discussion and debate once learners have progressed beyond the beginning level.

Satellite television also allows access to some 'free' structured language series, used to sell the accompanying book.

Interactive video

Finally, a potentially excellent tool for language learning in business is that of interactive video, which combines the computer with video to allow independent, autonomous, self-paced language learning. Most of the software development has so far been in English as a foreign language, and the price of hardware has yet to settle at economic levels, but materials suitable for business use in other languages are beginning to emerge. Interactive programmes can also be broadcast via satellite television during off-peak times. On the technical front laservision, digital and compact disc (CD-ROM or CD-I) technology contribute vastly improved sound and picture quality alongside sophisticated random access techniques, though consumer applications are still few and far between (see also chapters 5 & 7).

CONCLUSION

In summary, TV and video-based materials can help you to achieve your primary business aim by helping staff to build confidence in their interpersonal communication skills and their ability to adapt to different cultures and languages. They can demonstrate the relevance of language learning to the real world of business and work, and can prove an enjoyable and effective way of accessing foreign languages and cultures. 'Non-language learners' particularly will benefit and make progress, given time, commitment and organisation.

As we have seen, such media bring to the learning process unique qualities, especially if they form part of an overall pro-language learning culture and strategy within the company. They are particularly good for staff motivation: getting people started, and helping them to keep going when the going gets tough.

Learning technology has been identified as one of six broad variables determining the rate of success in language learning in chapter 3. A TV or video course, when successfully incorporated into variable 1 (course structure), and with the informed, sympathetic and active support of variable 6 (the tutor), can play a major role in positively influencing the characteristics of variable 5: the learner – his or her aptitude, motivation, attitude and personality (see pages 61–2).

All in all, language learning and training in the UK are at an exciting turning point. TV/video are without doubt poised to play a key role, now and in the future.

Checklist of main points

- TV/video are an essential part of an effective language learning and training strategy for business.
- TV promotes awareness, alters perceptions, challenges monoglot cultural assumptions and motivates millions to study by bringing foreign languages and cultures into the home.
- Video develops language skills and cultural insights by bringing a piece of the country into the classroom, office or open learning centre.
- They are most effective when integrated with a multi-media package.
- They are most effective within a dual strategy: tutor base and open learning.
- TV/video replicate the experience of 'being there', lending meaning, purpose and credibility to the language learning process.
- Proper technical back-up and trained tutor provision are essential to the successful corporate use of TV/video.
- 'Appointment systems' promote regular effective media-centred learning.
- Video and ancillary materials suitable for business language learning are on the increase: selection criteria are crucial.
- Media-based language learning impacts upon the four variables for success.

CHAPTER TEN

BUSINESS CULTURE TRAINING

BILL REED

BUSINESS CULTURE TRAINING AND THE INTEGRATED LANGUAGE STRATEGY

- Typical needs • Filling in the gaps in the language training policy

BUSINESS CULTURE TRAINING

- What is it? • Know yourself • Learn something • Be yourself

SUMMARY

BUSINESS CULTURE TRAINING AND THE INTEGRATED LANGUAGE STRATEGY

Typical needs

When our fictional company Carruthers & Co. set out on this route to internationalisation, they had to take some pretty hard-nosed decisions, as we have seen in the preceding chapters. They came up against one or two questions, though, that didn't quite fit with the integrated language strategy they had begun to develop:

> 'Tom Smith is making good progress in his German, but the German market is looking less and less attractive. Where

should he be going to look for business now? And do they speak German there?'

'Arnold Morgan's Italian is now getting really good, but he's hardly ever been there. The last time he went, he came back frustrated beyond belief at "the way they do things over there" and with the system still not agreed. He's a brilliant systems consultant in the UK, but his skills don't seem to translate. How long will it take him to learn the do's and don'ts of successful business in Italy?'

'Susanna Jones is in Export Marketing. In the course of her working year, she gets to visit over a dozen different countries – from Japan to Peru, from Dubai to Denmark. And her staff all have dealings with these countries albeit from a home base. It's simply impossible to learn all these languages, and yet each country seems to call for a different approach. What can we do to give ourselves the best chance of success in these markets?'

'In fact, there is a stratum of middle managers in Carruthers & Co., all of whom are fairly competent in their various fields, but who have never had to apply their skills in an international context. What problems are they likely to encounter now that we are going full steam ahead, and what can we do about it?'

Filling in the gaps in the language training policy

Language training is of course a crucial element in developing business long term in any specific territory. You simply won't be taken seriously otherwise. But there are a few gaps left at the margins of a language training policy: gaps that business culture training fills.

What are these gaps? Firstly, learning a language to a level at which you can contemplate working in it (selling, talking about products, negotiating, leading a team) takes a long time. A reasonable estimate might be something in the region of 300 hours of intensive group or individual work to get from zero to a level at which you might be comfortable in simple one-to-one meetings in a given language. And that supposes plenty of home study and revision, perhaps over an 18-month period. It's a serious medium-term commitment for any busy manager. The point is, you may *have* to be doing business in Paris *before* your rusty school French has turned into a shining sword of commerce.

Secondly, once you *have* made the grade in a particular language, your new-found ability to *speak* fluently to your Paraguayan counterpart does not guarantee that you are communicating with him. Just like a Brit on his first trip to the Kentucky subsidiary, you are speaking the same language, but not speaking the same language. You still need to know what makes that Paraguayan businessman tick, what his values are, how he prefers to do business.

Thirdly, there is a limit to the number of languages that any busy manager can have a go at, and that limit may well be lower than the number of countries the company wants to do business with. So, as well as being complementary to language training, business culture training can act as a replacement in urgent cases or where the expenditure of time and money could not be justified in business terms. It's often 'next best thing' or 'bare minimum'.

Fourthly, business culture training can make a substantial contribution to issues of international teamwork. 'Working with the Japanese' might be a more useful addition to the training offered within a multinational company (obviously where there is a Japanese company in the group) than 'How to sell to Japanese buyers'. Of course, British subsidiaries of foreign companies have many needs in this area.

Fifthly, success for Arnold Morgan might well mean that some day soon he will get the job of running the Italian subsidiary. His grasp of Italian will be fine, his understanding of how the Italians do business will have been enhanced by his business culture training sessions. But what about Italian tax? What kind of health service is there in Milan? Schooling for the kids? Will his wife be able to work? Briefing on living in different cultures also forms a part of the necessary preparation for Arnold – that is, if he doesn't want to waste the first six months of his assignment.

Expressions of need for business culture training

- It takes a long time to learn French – I need to do business there now!
- I speak the language but don't know what makes them tick.
- I can't possibly learn the languages of all the cultures I have to visit.
- We talk in fluent English, but we don't yet work as a team.
- I'm moving there next week, I need a survival guide on the nitty gritty (housing, health, insurance).

These are the primary reasons for companies providing business culture training to their staff. A good business culture training provider will be able to offer intensive, practical and, most of all, relevant solutions to particular needs such as those above. In one case, my company prepared a team for a major international exhibition by providing an audiocassette to raise the issues, training workshops to make them real and reading matter for follow-up and consolidation. In another, we prepared a sales team for their assault on the European market. In yet another, our brief was to help British managers come to a better working understanding of their new Japanese bosses.

BUSINESS CULTURE TRAINING

What is it?

But what is it? What is the nature of such training? How long does it take? Speaking as a supplier of such training, my answer to the last question has to be 'the length of a piece of string'; my answer to the first, 'it depends on what you really want to get out of it'. That said, let's try to break it down into useful component parts.

Can one generalize about the objectives of business culture training? Probably not, but here goes anyway: the main aim is to go some way towards being as effective in one's business dealings across cultural boundaries as on home ground. To achieve progress in that aim, the best formula I know is:

- know yourself;

- learn something; and
- be yourself.

Know yourself

How often do we really challenge the way we do things round here? We are all resistant to change and find comfort in the familiar. In business, those who have worked only in the UK may well be forgiven for thinking that the British way is the only way. One of the first targets of business culture training is to demonstrate that there *are* other ways of doing things. 'OK,' replies the true Brit, 'I can see some differences in their approach to their life and their work; some are more industrious than us, some are lazier; some are colder than us, some are over-friendly. But, all in all, when you come down to it, we've probably got it just about right. The British way may not be the only way. It's just the best way!'

It is common to find what is 'normal for me' being expressed in terms of 'best' – it's another lunge for the comfort zone. However, a quick look at the success of, say, the Japanese and the German economies normally inspires a touch more humility on this point. The Brit might accept the notion that 'best' needs defining, and that ultimately our way of doing business is just one way among many. Not better, not worse, just different.

Another question is: To what extent are you, the participant, typical of your culture? In what way do you differ from some arbitrary norms? And what are these norms? Do they have any real meaning?

What is your attitude to work? To your boss? To business in general? Is loyalty to your family more important than to your company? To your country? Are these bonds more important than telling the truth? Do you ever tell white lies to protect people's feelings? 'Time is money' or 'Gather ye rosebuds . . .'?

These and many other questions form an important first step in business culture training. Discussion of these matters establishes that there are many valid ways of running one's life that don't look too much like one's own. It establishes that one's own culture is not an absolute from which all others are in some way deviant, rather that it is relative to all the rest, just one point along many different scales, more 'this' than some, less 'that' than others.

> For Susanna Jones (our globe-trotting heroine of Export Marketing), this part of the programme involves a simple exercise in ranking the importance to herself of half a dozen well-known proverbs, and then being as honest as she can be in talking the rest of her working group through her answers (of course, she could have opted for one-to-one training, but she was persuaded by the arguments of group dynamics and synergy, especially where such attitudinal matters are concerned).

While still on the subject of assumptions and prejudices, we might consider how we are seen by other cultures. If we imagined the preconceptions held by, say, an Arab, we might list in his ideas of a typical Brit such adjectives as 'imperialist', 'arrogant', 'uncultured', 'impatient', 'irreligious'. If we did the same for a New Yorker, we might see things like 'slow', 'old-fashioned', 'polite', etc. This confirms the points made earlier about 'normality' – it all depends on the viewpoint. We recognise these stereotypes of the British as perhaps out-of-date and unduly negative, but we cannot deny that they do exist. Does this tell us anything about *our* views of these cultures – could *we* be out-of-date in *our* views? More importantly, if we are keen to create a good impression of ourselves, our company and our culture, do the results of this type of exercise give us any tips on how to avoid confirming the worst, how to make sure the impression is more positive?

You will note that there are far more questions than answers in this section. That is entirely as it should be.

Learn something

What do you know about the Outer Mongolians? Not much, probably. What are the images conjured up? Perhaps, the yak, the lonely herdsman in his strange tent on vast expanses of cold-looking scrubland, the high cheekbones. Not much of a picture. It's a primitive model of a culture and little help in thinking about how you might do business with them. But at least it's something.

Now think about the Spaniards. How much more developed is

that model? You have probably got a lot more data contributing to the picture; perhaps from business trips to the country, from personal acquaintances, from reading, from television, from school geography lessons, etc.

These models are a lot more use to us than those stereotypes referred to above. Whereas a stereotype is old, negative, backward-looking and fixed, a model is a flexible framework, albeit a far from perfect one, to which more learning can be applied. It can be developed and enriched during the course of business culture training and allows continuous development after the programme, as real experiences are added to the growing model.

But here we need something of a health warning: these models are like economists' statistical models; and like all statistics they are necessarily flawed. They are useful for analysing the past, and the best we can do at predicting general trends in the future; what they can never do is predict any specific, individual event. Another way of looking at it is: if you roll a dice 600 times, it is likely that you will get somewhere near 100 sixes. However, the chances of getting a six with the 601st throw are still five to one against. What this means in business culture training terms is simple: it is a racing certainty that, after we have worked for several days on your model of a typical Swedish businessman, the next Swede you meet will contradict all that you have learnt. The message: *you do business with people, not with models – however sophisticated and refined.*

So how do you actually go about developing and enriching your model? Again, I believe there is a simple process that gives us a memorable framework to build upon:

Facts > Attitudes > Behaviour > Communication

What are the significant *facts* about, say, the Hungarian culture that affect what it is like to *be* Hungarian? How have the facts created the range of *attitudes* prevalent in that culture? How are those attitudes reflected in the *behaviour* of Hungarians and the idiosyncrasies of doing business there? And, on the basis of all that, what advice is there on how one should modify one's style of *communication* when trying to work with Hungarians? This last section assumes of course that the managers on the programme will not really be able to justify the time it would take to learn Hungarian.

So, the *facts* might be historico-political – modern-day Hungarians can hardly fail to be affected by the last 45 years. They might be geographical – Hong Kong is a harbour more than an island; what does that tell us about the HK Chinese? The facts might be demographic – Japan has been over-populated for centuries, there is no word in Japanese for 'privacy'. The important thing is that the facts should be significant, adding substantially to the building blocks of the model.

The *attitudes* may well be explained by the facts, but that's still some way from their being acceptable or assimilable. In many cases, the differences in approach to what we regard as the basic structures of our thinking can be hard to take: radically different attitudes to daughters, pragmatic approaches to telling the truth, putting the family last. We cannot and should not try to adopt these attitudes for ourselves; rather we can begin to appreciate why these attitudes exist. It is important always to remember that this 'weird way of doing things' makes good sense to the culture in question. If it didn't, the culture would not have survived. Or perhaps it won't survive much longer!

Moving into 'real-time' dealings with other cultures, *behaviour* patterns (or at least recognition thereof) can easily be learnt. Body language can be harmonised with counterparts. Most people know about the gaffes you can make in dealings with exotic cultures – showing the soles of your feet, slapping backs, eye-balling, etc. Business culture training can train out the gaffes and train in the 'brownie points', i.e. those things you can do to make a positive impression on your foreign partner.

Typical examples of gaffes and of creating the wrong impression are:

> *Eye-balling*: The 'honest-broker' Brit deals eye-to-eye with his Bangkok agent; he wonders if he can trust this person who is squirming at the other end of the table and 'refusing' to meet his level gaze. The Thai is feeling utterly discomforted by the intrusive stare of his principle – does he have no respect for me and my compatriots? How can he be so rude?

The left hand: Arnold Morgan, on an exploratory sortie to the Middle East, found that the initial warm welcome he received seemed to curdle on a number of occasions. The problem: Arnold is left-handed. He tends to favour the left hand in everything he does, including handing over papers, brochures, samples, etc. The Saudi, a man of the world, fully appreciates that Westerners often are unaware that the left hand in many parts of the world is reserved mainly for cleansing purposes. Nevertheless, he cannot help, at a subconscious level, feeling somehow deeply uneasy ... slightly tainted ... just slightly unclean.

The business card: True story: an American banker walked into the offices of Mitsubishi Bank in Tokyo and introduced himself to his host. His host naturally presented his *meishi* (business card). The American: 'Sorry, I only got in last night, I don't have any cards.' So, he tore in half the card he had just received, scribbled his name and telephone number on it and handed it back to the shocked Japanese banker.

First name: An English manager, on one of his first trips to Germany, was encouraged by the warmth of his reception in the Bonn subsidiary. So, in the restaurant that evening, with his counterpart, his counterpart's boss and his counterpart's assistant, he said: 'Look, let's forget this Mr Jenkins stuff, call me Norman – and you're Hans, you're Uli and you're Stefan, right?' The Germans knew that was the way in the UK, but resented what came across as an HQ cultural imposition – we do things differently here, we feel more comfortable doing things the German way.

The remaining problem is *communication*. If we accept business culture training as a pragmatic alternative to language training, what can we do to improve communication? Here we need to start by making an assumption. Despite what some might say, the most common language of international business is English. A very large part of the world's business is done in one form of English or another, and there is no reason to suppose that things will change significantly over the next 30 or 40 years. The question is: what sort of English is it? Let's take an example.

When Ciba Geigy run a meeting in Basel with four Swiss managers, two French, two Italians, one Japanese and one Englishman, they speak English. In this meeting, who is the one at the most disadvantage linguistically? Is it the Japanese – far from his own culture and by no means the most competent active speaker of English? Maybe. Is it the French with a certain vestigial resistance to having to speak English and their awful pronunciation problems? Possibly. But equally it could be the Brit. He may well find himself isolated as the only native speaker of the language. The others all share another language: Offshore English.

Offshore English is the English that the Frenchman speaks to the German, the Korean to the Turk. It is slightly defective in that its speakers often share the same grammatical mistakes (but then is it really a 'mistake' if they both make it?). It is rather boring, since all the spice that we love so well, the idiom that makes Arthur Daley distinguishable from Bertie Wooster, is missing. Subtle it is not; effective as a means of business communication it most certainly is.

Foreign managers that I have spoken to over the past decade confirm some nasty impressions: the British speak English too fast, too idiomatically, they waffle, they use their superiority as a weapon (a bit of paranoia, a bit of truth?), and they never listen or try to understand what I am saying in my broken English. Result: a breakdown not only in communication but also in the relationship. It's hardly going to help Carruthers & Co. sell their way into another market.

> This breakdown is evidenced by the policy of several well-known continental European companies (notable among them is Pirelli) who refuse to employ native English-speaking management trainers or consultants. They prefer the Dutchman or the Swiss who speaks excellent offshore English. Similarly, a large Finnish company recently selected a French, rather than a British joint-venture partner – 'because we can understand their English better'.

Business culture training can and does make significant progress in eradicating these tendencies in the British manager. This

F→A→B→C process consists of what we call an 'active briefing session'.

The primary need is for clarity at all costs. Putting any Brit on video in a simple role-play and then playing back to him some of his deficiencies in this area normally has a dramatic effect.

Taking Arnold Morgan, our Italian-speaking systems consultant: he would spend up to a day in a small group being encouraged by the trainer to supply the building blocks to the model that they are developing – i.e. all those things he already knows about Italy and the way Italians do business. The trainer would complete the picture by enriching the model through passing on his own knowledge and experience. Hardly a lecture, though; more a group discussion.

Within a couple of days, real progress can be made – and, according to people who have gone through it, the messages stick.

This communication skills element of the training naturally extends to such areas as presentation and negotiation skills. Cultural awareness will certainly have a significant effect when the manager considers the audience for his next presentation. And it is almost axiomatic to observe that negotiating with a Spanish managing director is radically different from negotiating with a dozen Chinese. In the first case, an intimate developing of personal trust and mutual understanding precedes and permits the move into serious number-crunching; but the relationship comes first. In the second case, the skills of persistence, tenacity and stamina need to be applied in the face of occasionally aggressive questioning from all sides at once. Success in this may well lead to the development of good relationships – but the deal comes first – and you have to prove yourself worthy of their respect. This focused, culture-specific negotiation training is perhaps the single most popular service that we (and others, of course) provide to our market.

Be yourself

The training I have tried to describe above should ideally be highly intensive, practical and relevant. On occasions, it can have a quite profound effect on the participants. I have seen people who so take on board the message about the need for flexibility, sensitivity and an appreciation of the other culture's point of view that their final role-play shows them as 'more German than the Germans'; they have empathised so well with the target culture that they have nearly become one of them. This sets all the alarm bells ringing. It simply doesn't work, of course.

No culture likes being too closely copied. Feeling flattered by admirers is one thing, feeling that someone is intruding on home ground is quite another. In Japan, for example, you are *expected* to find some of the more exotic food not quite to your taste, and you are regarded as slightly suspect if your command of Japanese is *too* good.

The main message at the end of business culture training is 'Be yourself'. You can't successfully be anyone else. You are rooted in your culture whether you like it or not. Indeed, I believe that you cannot be truly international without some deep affinity for your own culture; the alternative, the rootless lowest-common-denominator, so-called 'Hilton culture' is more like shallow cosmopolitanism.

The true learner from business culture training leaves the programme with greater cultural self-knowledge, an enriched understanding of the territories in question and the sensitivity to behaviour and communication issues which will ensure maximum effectiveness in doing business across the cultural divide. These atttributes together with a growing facility in the language make a formidable combination and, at the level of the individual, go a long way towards ensuring optimum success in international business.

SUMMARY

As a company develops its international business, it needs international managers. Fitting inside or around the edges of an integrated language training policy, business culture training has an important contribution to make.

The need:
• urgent cases (the language lessons continue);

- filling in the picture (what makes them tick);
- too many territories (a language too far . . .);
- international teamwork (business efficiency); and
- 'survival' (the cost of soap powder).

The process:

- know yourself (norms and stereotypes);
- learn something (model-building; facts → attitudes → behaviour; communication; offshore English; presentations; negotiating across cultures); and
- be yourself (roots and the Hilton culture).

The result:

- freedom from trauma (culture shock);
- brownie points in place of gaffes; and
- progress towards the 'international manager'.

CHAPTER ELEVEN

TRANSLATING AND INTERPRETING

GEOFFREY KINGSCOTT

TRANSLATING

- 'False friends'

HOW TO OBTAIN TRANSLATIONS

- What to avoid • Translating and interpreting are different skills • Professional bodies and standards • How to use a translation provider and what to look for

INTERPRETING

- Types of interpreter

THE 'QUALITY' ISSUE

TRANSLATING

A celebrated example of the difficulties of translation is that apparently most simple of English phrases, 'The cat sat on the mat'. Try putting that into French or German, or any language with which you are familiar. You cannot do so without stating in what manner the cat is sitting, or whether the action was momentary or over a period of time; and you need to know what sort of mat it was. The complications are endless, and are a good illustration that translation is not as simple as it may seem.

Of course, say the wiseacres, but while this might be true of everyday or literary language, in technical language nuts and bolts are nuts and bolts. Try telling that to a technical translator. In German a bolt maybe a *Schraube* (a word also used for 'screw') or a *Bolzen*, possibly even a *Stift*, depending on the characteristics of the bolt in question. In French a 'valve' can be a *soupape*, a *clapet* or a *vanne*, occasionally even a *valve*, depending on its function and the way it operates.

Because, and this is the point that has to be made time and time again, the concept being very difficult for the non-linguist layman to grasp, translation is not just a matter of word-for-word substitution. If it were, it would all have been done by the computers long ago.

The truth is that different languages, even those as closely related as English, French and German, see the world and identify and describe reality in a different way. To a Frenchman, there is no generic word covering every type of valve: he differentiates automatically between a device of the check-valve type (*clapet*), of the gate-valve type (*vanne*), or the types operated by balls, needles, slides, etc. (*soupape*).

Europeans find English odd in that we only have one word, 'know', for what they consider two entirely separate concepts, to be acquainted with (*connaître* in French, *kennen* in German), and to know as a fact or how to do something, (*savoir* in French, *wissen* in German).

Hundreds of examples of such different ways of looking at the world could be quoted, and indeed whole books have been written on the subject (see, for example, Vinay and Darbelnet's classic study, *Stylistique comparée du français et de l'anglais*).

'False friends'

Everyone has seen examples of the hilarious results when one language is translated literally from another, of the type 'We went to Buckingham Palace to see the guards relieving themselves' (*se relever*), or one that I came across at a town twinning ceremony I attended (the English text had been done by the teacher of English in the local lycée), 'After the ceremony there will be a defiling (*une défilée*) of the fire brigade'. The word *gai* is frequently used in French in all sorts of contexts, and Frenchmen speaking English in the current context frequently lay themselves open to mis-understandings when they translate it literally. Translating in the other direction, Englishmen often use when speaking French the verb *exciter* without realising it often has connotations in French of sexual arousal. It is said that the actor Gérard Depardieu, who played the leading role in the film *Cyrano de Bergerac*, would have got an Oscar if he had not told an interviewer of an incident when, as a child, he had had the misfortune of being unwittingly present at a rape. Unfortunately he used the French verb *assister à* meaning 'to be present at', but this was wrongly translated as 'assist' and his character was thereby blackened beyond redemption.

Terms which are apparently so similar between one language and another, but which have taken on different meanings, are called 'false friends' by linguists, and here again whole books have been devoted to the subject.

Even words which are directly borrowed from one language to another change their meaning almost immediately. The English seized on the German word *Blitzkrieg* in the Second World War, but instead of applying it in the German sense, to a strategy of attack using fast-moving armoured columns to penetrate a front and strike deep into the enemy rear, the English applied it to an intense raid on one location. The French borrowed the term *le marketing*, but applied it more to what we would call market research than to actually publicising and selling the goods. The Germans borrowed the word 'oldtimer' and use it as their standard term for what we call a veteran car.

HOW TO OBTAIN TRANSLATIONS

What to avoid

The company buyer must be aware, therefore, that translation is full of pitfalls for the unwary, and is not to be entrusted to anyone who claims to be able to speak another language. All too frequently when the translation problem arises resort is made to the first person one can think of who has foreign language knowledge – the 'bilingual secretary', the French teacher at the local school, the 'Polish chap in the works who speaks six languages', or the German-born wife of a colleague. Such actions are dangerous, because the persons concerned are probably deluded about their ability.

For example, take someone born in Germany who has lived in England for many years. While still able to communicate in German without difficulty, he or she is probably out of touch with the terms used in the modern language. I remember a German lady of this type maintaining stoutly that the German word for 'holidays' was always *Ferien*, and I was being perverse in stating that *Urlaub* – a word which originally had connotations of military leave – was now the more common in the context we were dealing with. Only by producing German holiday brochures and advertisements, all of which used *Urlaub*, could I convince her of the change in language usage. It is not that she had not visited Germany during her years in England, where people would have accepted and understood what she said without demur, it is just that she was not sensitive to language change.

New concepts, new devices, new trends are appearing all the time. If you have to translate terms such as 'bottle bank', 'food court' or 'heritage centre', you cannot afford to make up literal equivalents: these would probably make no sense to the reader. You have to find out what words are being used for these concepts in the actual country. Once again, literal translation, or just guessing, are worse than useless.

It is, in short, a false economy to have translation or interpreting done by anyone who is not a professional translator or interpreter.

Translating and interpreting are different skills

At this stage we ought to draw a clear distinction between translation and interpreting. Strictly speaking, translation is concerned with the written word (text), and interpreting with the spoken word (speeches or discourse). In practice, the layman often confuses the two – a television interview with a foreigner, for example, may flash up the words 'Voice of translator' to make it clear that it is not the interviewee himself who is speaking English; what they really should state is 'Voice of interpreter'. In the language professions, however, the correct distinction between translation and interpreting is always drawn, and you could cause confusion by using the terms wrongly.

Professional bodies and standards

How, then, does one find a professional translator or interpreter when the need arises?

Here again we have a problem, and it is this. Anyone can call him or herself a translator, whether competent or not. When you get in touch with a plumber, a solicitor or an architect, you know they are going to have a certain minimum level of qualification, because they would otherwise not be allowed to exercise their profession. But no such compulsory qualification exists for the professions of translator and interpreter.

Furthermore, many people in the UK who call themselves translators are not working to a professional standard, and are often blithely ignorant of their inadequacies. This also applies to translation companies. There are some good translators, and some good translation companies, and the first problem is to separate the gold from the dross.

As in so many fields (cf. travel agents, builders, electrical engineers) membership of a professional association, while not providing a foolproof guarantee, does at least indicate a measure of commitment to the profession and aspiration to levels of quality.

The principal body to which most full-time practitioners of translation in the UK belong, especially technical translators, is the **Institute of Translation and Interpreting** (ITI), founded in 1983, who can be contacted at 318a Finchley Road, London NW3 5HT, telephone 071–794 9931, facsimile 071–435 2105. Literary translators, who usually work directly for publishers, tend to belong to another body, the **Translators Association** (TA) of the Society of Authors, but the ITI and the TA work in close collaboration. The ITI and the TA are the UK associations affiliated to the international federation of translators – the **Fédération Internationale des Traducteurs** (FIT).

Qualified members of the ITI are entitled to put MITI (Member of the ITI) or FITI (Fellow of the ITI) after their names. Qualification is by a combination of examination, assessment, length of experience, and references. A directory of members, or names of translators suitable for a particular application, can be obtained from the ITI office. If the ITI is unable to suggest a name, perhaps because the language combination or the subject specialisation is unusual, they may suggest you get in touch with their sister organisation in the country of your target language. Do not be shy of sending translation work out of the country; the best place for a translator to be located is in the country of his target language, and in these days when facsimiles and modems are connecting up the whole world, it pays to operate internationally.

A more venerable body (founded in 1910) is the **Institute of Linguists** (IoL), best known for its language examinations, whose membership is drawn from all types of linguist, divided up into divisions according to types of activity. One of the divisions is a translation division, and one of the IoL's examinations is for a Diploma in Translation (DipTrans). The IoL, which has associate status with the FIT, publishes a directory of its members who engage in translation activity.

How to use a translation provider and what to look for

It is much, much safer to use directories of qualified translators than to resort to Yellow Pages or the lists kept by such institutions as libraries, chambers of commerce, etc., which have no means of checking the credentials of applicants.

It is very difficult to find *experienced translators* who are prepared to come and work on your premises on a short-term placement basis. Your full-time freelance operates quite a high-powered little business, and is like a fish out of water if forced to operate away from his well-equipped office, just as your solicitor or architect would be.

That does not mean that the translator should not visit you, to discuss a translation project, to familiarise himself with your products and procedures, or to deliver work. But it may be more instructive for you to visit the translator, and see just how well equipped he is to tackle your work.

A professional translator will supply work typed to a presentation standard, usually produced using a word processing program on a personal computer, and printed on a laser printer. Often the work can be supplied on disk. There are still a lot of problems with system and format compatibility, even when saving documents in ASCII, but with goodwill and openness on both sides these can usually be overcome. If you are inputting the material into a company desktop publishing system, you should be aware that some DTP systems are not very good at handling foreign language hyphenation, particularly in German.

You should be aware that while you may find a translator translating into English who can translate from more than one foreign language (Translator X may translate into English from French, Italian and Spanish, and Translator Y may translate into English from German and Dutch, for example), when translating out of English into other languages you will need one translator for each target language. This is because a professional translator translates *only* into his mother tongue. Thus anyone resident in the UK who translates into French will normally have had a French parentage, and have come to this country after an upbringing and education in a French-speaking country. Only a comparatively small handful of translators are recognised by the translator associations as being genuinely bilingual.

As a glance at Yellow Pages will show, in addition to freelance translators there are also a large number of translation companies, all clamouring for your business. There are some excellent translation companies in the UK, but there are also many companies whose standards of quality and performance are inadequate. Many of the inadequate ones are merely what is called in the trade 'envelope-changing agencies', that is, they take the work out of the envelope from the customer and put it in an envelope which they send to a freelance, and then reverse the process a week or two later when the job is finished.

It is therefore always a good idea not only to take up references when engaging a translation company, but also to visit their premises. All translation companies will use specialist freelances to a greater or lesser extent, but you should expect to see enough linguists on the full-time staff to allow outside work to be checked and processed. Ask some pointed questions: for example, how will they cope with the specialist terminology of your particular industry, what reference material do they have at their disposal, what are the linguistic qualifications of the staff who organise the translations?

Once again, though not a foolproof safeguard, membership of a professional association is an indication of a certain commitment to professional standards. The ITI, mentioned above, also has a separate category of 'corporate members', and can supply a list of the translation companies who have been admitted as such. There is also an **Association of Translation Companies** (ATC), which maintains a permanent office at 7 Buckingham Gate, London SW1E 6JS, telephone 071–630 5454, facsimile 071–630 5767.

Can't it all be done by computer, anyway?

Automatic translation by computer can work, in certain limited circumstances, and where the whole documentation process, including the generation of original text, is very tightly controlled.

But there is no magic machine which will take your English documents and, as it were, produce a French 'photocopy' at the touch of a button.

Experts have been working on automatic translation by computer, known in the language business as *machine translation* (MT), for over 40 years, and some interesting advances have been made. It is a subject in which I have long taken a close personal interest. At present, MT accounts for only a tiny fraction of world translation activity, but that fraction will grow as more and more organisations and companies get their whole documentation process, including the original technical writing, re-organised on a highly controlled and integrated basis. If you have a large and homogenous throughput of work, it might be worth looking at the MT solution in the long term, but it will almost certainly take you a year or two of hard work and careful planning to build an efficient system which is as good as human translation and can show significant gains in cost and production time.

For the one-off and occasional applications which are required by most companies, the MT route is not yet economic, nor is there usually time to apply it.

It is becoming increasingly recognised that translation is not an independent activity, but one facet of document production. And often it is not just a case of straight translation. Documents obtained for information purposes may need to be summarised, or selectively translated. In other circumstances the straight translation, just rendering the meaning of a text into the target language, may be only the first step to what is required. This is particularly true in the case of texts for advertising, which is why a separate chapter is devoted to this topic.

INTERPRETING

Types of interpreter

There are very few people outside the exalted ranks of conference interpreters who earn a full-time living from interpreting. This means that when you want someone to interpret for you at your factory or on an exhibition stand, the person concerned will also be engaged in other activities, such as translation or language teaching, when they are not working as an interpreter. But not all translators are good at interpreting – the two activities require different skills, and a somewhat different personality – and people who are good at interpreting sometimes make poor translators.

Conference interpreters, as I have hinted, are a breed apart. Sometimes called simultaneous interpreters, these are the people who sit in glass-fronted booths at the back of the conference hall and interpret into a microphone everything they hear as soon as it is spoken. The delegates in the hall listen to the interpretation in their own language over headphones.

Many people associate simultaneous interpreting only with international organisations, such as the United Nations or the European Parliament, but it is possible to hire portable equipment and set it up anywhere. Industrial firms making a presentation to foreign dealers or buyers often use such facilities. Conference interpreters see themselves as an elite, and charge accordingly. Their elitism is justified by the difficulty of what they do. If you do not think it is difficult, try listening to the television news and, as it is being broadcast, paraphrase aloud what is being said. You will find two things: first, that it is difficult to keep up with the speaker and not to lose the thread of the discourse, and, second, that you are disconcerted by the sound of your own voice – to listen and speak at the same time requires tremendous powers of concentration. For this reason conference interpreters usually work in pairs, one pair for each language direction, and relieve one another every 20 minutes or so.

Most conference interpreters belong to the **Association internationale des interprètes de conférence** (AIIC), which has its headquarters at 10 avenue de Sécheron, 1211 Genève, Switzerland, telephone +41 22 731 3323, facsimile +41 22 732 4151. AIIC will provide you with names and addresses of conference interpreters available in the UK, and one member of AIIC will usually agree to recruit the rest of the team. Members of AIIC will not usually work with non-professionals, so you should forget the idea of getting your 'bilingual secretary' to fill one of the slots on the basis that 'the experience will do her good'.

Consecutive interpreting requires an interpreter to sit or stand alongside the speaker, and to interpret what has been said after the speaker has finished speaking, and is sometimes used for formal speeches, presentations, etc. Even with note-taking, the technique requires formidable powers of memory.

Whispered interpreting is where there are one or two persons only in an audience who speak a language different to that of the speakers; the interpreter whispers the interpretation into their ears. It is sometimes used in court cases.

In most cases, however, where a firm needs an interpreter, it is to facilitate communication with one or more foreign visitors throughout the day, in various types of situation: at the airport, across the boardroom table, visiting the works, inspecting the plant, over meals, etc. This is usually known as *liaison interpreting* or *ad hoc interpreting*.

Few people make a full time freelance living as liaison interpreters, and this work is usually done by linguists whose main occupation is in other fields, such as translation. And when engaging an interpreter, you should look for the same sort of qualification as for a translator.

THE 'QUALITY' ISSUE

This chapter has provided you with information or the processes of professional translating and interpreting. Within the context of 'quality' requirements of your organisation and within the framework of any language strategy or policy it is a false economy to have translation or interpreting done by anyone who is not a professional translator or interpreter. The next chapter deals with the production of foreign language advertising texts and documents, an area which sometimes *involves* translation as one of the processes but which, in many other ways, is a separate issue.

CHAPTER TWELVE

FOREIGN LANGUAGE 'PUBLICITY' MATERIAL

DOUG EMBLETON

HOW TO MISS BY A MILE

- Some typical examples • Reasons to be careful

WHAT EXACTLY IS 'PUBLICITY' MATERIAL?

- Categories • 'Quality'

'IT'S SIMPLY A MATTER OF TRANSLATING ISN'T IT?'

- Some guidelines on appropriate routes

QUALITY CONTROL AND THE 'MIRROR EFFECT'

- The stages involved and who should be involved • 'The mirror effect' • What does 'getting it wrong' entail?

CULTURAL/MARKET ADAPTATION

- The obvious • The not so obvious

PRIORITIES AND DEADLINES

- Why cut the Quality cloth? • 'Mr Reasonable'

CAN COMPUTERS HELP?

- Maximise their potential • Limitations

HOW TO 'MISS BY A MILE'

Some typical examples

From the packaging of a 'marker pen' produced in Japan:

'At the using:
1 Use after shaking well.
2 Instant dry! cap on the head after using.

*Feature
1 Particular pen nib so unique feeling in writing matchless in steady and wearproof.
2 White oilily ink having cubic effect is no change of quality in variation of season.
3 The container having special constitution can be written as far as the last drop.'

Extracts from instructions for using a frying pan produced in Spain:

'Water . . . it must reach a level up to one centimetre of the frying-pan border with the supject, it be not poured out to boil.

A very important datum.—Once the rice have been poured, the frying pan must boil all equally. If the rice remains a little hard, water must not be added, no way. It is placed one white paper or one wet rag which covers the frying-pan and, in this form, it finish to be cooked. All this is attained, arranging the fire, in order to, it comes out dry and it does not remain hard.

Cooking with frying-pans . . . [trade name] *. . . you ha-ve the success insured.*'

Extracts from glossy advertising brochure for imported Japanese sake:

'Sake served warmed.

Japanese haven't gone nuts all suddenly Sake served

warmed but it has been the traditional way of drinking Sake for many hundred of years.

We are not stubborn as to suggest and insisting you to drink Sake warmed, you can try to drink chilled or on the rocks, and let you be the judge, which way you like the best.'

Reasons to be careful

These three texts are of 1960s vintage and form part of a collection which I have assembled over the years of examples of how *not* to get it quite right. However, they are not presented merely for amusement.

Imagine that one of them represents *your* product, service or organisation in another country. You would have been blissfully unaware of the errors or you would not have distributed copies . . . would you?

You believe in the quality of your organisation and its goods or services and you would flinch at these ever being depicted as faulty or second rate. That item of publicity or customer information will in many instances constitute *the* most permanent reminder of your organisation which its intended readership has available. You would like to imagine your customers finding all of the right information in the right places. In the best scenario, you imagine a potential new customer reaching for that glossy brochure or advert which created such a good impression and then picking up the telephone . . . and yet, it is surprising how often the production of such documents is relegated to an extremely low priority ranking.

Surprising, because the costs in time, effort and hard cash which are involved in ensuring that such documents really are of the desired quality are outweighed at least a thousand times over by the unseen but conceivably drastic costs of publicly and knowingly inflicting damage on your reputation and image.

'But that just wouldn't happen in our organisation.' Are you sure? In any case, the errors need not be so obvious as those quoted above for the potential damage to be just as severe. This chapter will help you to examine and implement various routes towards meeting the 'quality' objectives of publicity or advertising literature in foreign languages.

I was once talking to a printer who was delivering some materials to us. He told me of a local, small company which was about to market a very successful wallcovering product in Spain. Their printing requirements were very simple and inexpensive. A numbered list of five 'Instructions for Use'. These had been translated by somebody in the company who 'knew a bit of Spanish' and who had used a pocket dictionary. I often wondered how many quizzical looks this had possibly caused amongst any number of Spanish purchasers once they had stripped all their walls and were ready for action.

WHAT EXACTLY IS 'PUBLICITY' MATERIAL?

Cagetories

Advertising texts are seldom a mere matter of translation. They can involve catchphrases or a play on words.

Trade names can be a potential minefield as a thorough linguistic search has to be carried out to ensure that there are no equivalent words in other languages. Such equivalents have an undying habit of bordering on the obscene!

Exhibition display materials are similar to advertising texts in that they need to convey a sharp, concise message within a limited space.

Sales brochures describe a product or service and may also be of the 'corporate image' variety which describes the shape, size and basic *raison d'être* of an organisation.

Technical literature is usually aimed at downstream, industrial customers rather than end consumers. These documents will typically describe product specifications and properties, safety and handling procedures and product applications. Sales catalogues also come under this heading.

Consumer or end-user instructions are, for example, car manuals, operating instructions for brown goods (televisions, hi-fi systems, etc.) and for cameras, software, etc. – even wallpaper!

'Quality'

In one sense, they all have slightly differing objectives. Some are intended to inform, others to persuade. They also have many things in common because they represent a permanent reminder of:

- your product or service;
- your organisation;
- your image;
- your credibility as an acceptable supplier in the target market;
- your professionalism; and
- your reputation.

In short, they represent your *quality*.

'IT'S SIMPLY A MATTER OF TRANSLATING, ISN'T IT?'

Sometimes translation is involved as one of several stages. Sometimes it is not involved at all. It is *never* the sole ingredient! All the types of information listed above need to read as though they were written in the target country and, as such, need to read and project themselves as effectively as the equivalent documents which will undoubtedly be produced by the local competition.

At this point it is important to emphasise one of the golden rules of professional translating. The point has already been made that language training programmes are not designed to produce in-company translators. However, even within the maxim 'professional translaters do it for a full-time living' there resides a clear distinction between translations intended for the purpose of information within the organisation and translations which will be used in printed – and often 'prestigious' – documents aimed at overseas customers. Quite literally, professional translators translate *into their native tongue* and *within clearly defined subject areas*.

In other words,

- when a translation is appropriate, it should be carried out by a translator who is working into his or her mother tongue and who is also a subject expert;
- even then, other quality control checks are vital; and therefore
- whether the production of these types of document involves a translation of an original piece of English or a rewrite in the target language, the process is never simply a matter of translation.

Some guidelines on appropriate routes

The following guidelines can certainly be regarded as more than mere rules of thumb but, as you will discover in this chapter, there exists a range of circumstances which will govern the selection of the best method.

Advertisement texts never lend themselves to a strict translation from an original English text. Advertising and copywriting specialists in the target country are your safest bet.

Trade names are, in themselves, not a translation problem. Nonetheless, expert linguistic advice is called for to ensure that they do not offend.

Exhibition display materials and sales brochures can possibly be translated from original English texts but will still require other quality controls and cultural adaptations. As a general rule, they are best rewritten in the target country using the original English text as a reference point.

Technical literature and consumer/end-user instructions are the most 'translatable' types of text since they contain a more direct, technical language in the source text. They still require quality controls and cultural adaptation.

So, how far have we got?

- We have defined what constitutes 'publicity' material.
- Foreign language versions of publicity material should never involve a mere translation process.
- An awful lot is at stake for your organisation.

- Whoever handles the task must be a subject expert working into his or her native tongue.
- There are several quality control stages involved.

QUALITY CONTROL AND 'THE MIRROR EFFECT'

The stages involved and who should be involved

Again, we have to differentiate between documents which need to be rewritten or which require copywriting and documents which can involve translation as one of several stages.

Where a rewrite or copywriting is involved, a large organisation with overseas offices will naturally be guided by the local knowledge of its overseas PR experts. They will have access both to external advertising agencies and to the acceptable and 'in vogue' styles of advertising in the target country.

If translation of an original English text is appropriate as one of the stages then a large organisation should consider:

- cultural adaptation of the text in its English original; this is a vital starting point for an ultimately high quality document (see: 'Cultural and market adaptation' below);
- translation of the adapted text in the target country either by one of its in-house translation experts or by an approved external translation agency;
- a thorough check of the typed text by an in-house product or subject expert in the target country (do *not* leave any of these tasks to the proofreading stage – this simply adds to the total cost of the process). This really is an acid test, particularly if the checker is one of the people who will actually be handing the finished document over to customers;
- again at the typed text stage, a check of the text by an English mother tongue translation expert (see 'The mirror effect' below); and
- when – and only when – the final typed version is agreed should the text be printed. This can then become a relatively

speedy and inexpensive process (see 'Are computers of any use in this field?' below).

What about the small organisation with no overseas office or agent? Well, as mentioned in chapter 1, one really has to build up a relationship with an external provider which inspires one with confidence. A good checking mechanism is to ask how many of the above stages *they* will apply. Do not accept a 'just leave it all to us' response. If the document really is that important (and it must be, or you would not go to all of that expense, would you?), you can arrange to have the text checked by a second, independent checker. This could be somebody within your network of contacts or could involve even further expense, but the worst stage at which to find out that your literature is not up to scratch is when *x* thousand printed copies have been delivered – or worse still, when they have already been distributed to their intended readership.

> I recall once being called in to advise a small local company who were about to ship a whole batch of glossy, promotional brochures to South America for a prestigious exhibition. On the day of shipment I was asked to comment upon the texts. The very first sentence of the original English read: 'Company X has over 40 years' experience in overseas markets.' The foreign language version read: 'It is over 40 years since Company X has had any experience in overseas markets.' From then on, the foreign text went downhill! It had been produced as an all in one process by an agency and the customer had not been involved at any stage. This may not always be the case, but can you afford the risk?

The 'mirror effect'

The 'mirror effect' is not a complex theory. It is based on my many years of experience in this field. It simply explains that if a foreign language document is translated from an original English version it is only when an English mother tongue translation expert compares the two texts that potential ambiguities in the English or misunderstandings by the overseas translator become truly apparent. This is one of the most effective quality control mechanisms I know. It involves an extra stage and an extra person but is very revealing.

The process can be explained diagrammatically:

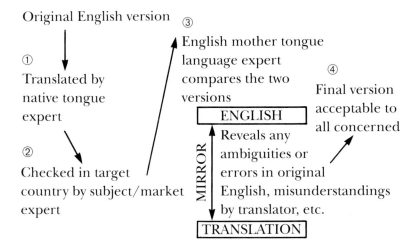

This is a fairly involved process but it does at least provide a thorough quality control and, in my experience, all of the individuals involved welcome this 'teamwork' approach. The process is not intended to be used by one party as a vehicle for criticism of another, and all the participants in the process need to understand that the ultimate objective is a finely polished final version. It is a form of international teamwork.

It may be viewed as a 'Rolls Royce' approach and it is true that it can work best in its entirety in a large organisation. However, in the case of a small- or medium-sized business the use of the 'mirror' stage on its own can be very effective. It can be reduced to arranging for a competent English mother tongue translator to translate back into English the foreign language version which has been prepared. This enables the small business to confirm that its foreign language 'publicity' puts across the intended message.

As the relationship between the participants or between an organisation and its provider of 'publicity' work develops, these stages can be diluted. However, in the early stages of producing publicity material in foreign languages the safety net and quality control offered by the 'mirror stage' are invaluable. We have already highlighted the costs of getting it wrong.

What does 'getting it wrong' entail?

Well, for example:

- the translation may be in wonderful prose but may be too literal;
- it may simply not convey the sort of message or style required;
- specialist jargon or terms unique to the organisation may not have been fully understood;
- the original English text may in fact have been too full of jargon and 'slick' terms which do not lend themselves to translation;
- the translator or overseas checker may have adapted the text or omitted sections based on their local market knowledge: these changes may be necessary but you need to know about them; and
- we *all* make mistakes – we are all human – and the 'mirror' process can pick these up in a non-incriminating way.

Above all, if the person within your organisation who is coordinating the whole process is not a linguist then it makes simple sense to have a 'mirror' check rather than to adopt a fingers-crossed; 'it looks foreign so it must be alright' approach.

> I once saw a glossy brochure which had been produced in German by a well-known, large British company. The short text had obviously been produced in a hurry by an overseas agent and sent by telex to the UK. The German 'umlaut' (ä, ö, ü) cannot be conveyed on telex equipment and is written in upper case as AE, OE, UE. The text, when printed in the UK, had been converted to lower case but the modified 'umlaut' had been retained. Over four glossy A4 pages it looked ridiculous.

CULTURAL/MARKET ADAPTATION

Texts can be culturally adapted or adapted to the conditions of the target market either in their original English form or during the translation and checking processes.

The obvious

The obvious items which can be adapted right from the start include:

- telephone numbers and addresses;
- units of measurement and calibration;
- references to standards or specifications (e.g. British Standard 'X' or 'under the Health & Safety Act (UK)' will have little impact or meaning in an overseas market); and
- are all of the products or properties also available in, or relevant to, the target market?

The not so obvious

The not so obvious items include:

- the actual typeface used: if the document is printed in the UK the typeface may seem odd in other countries;
- certain colours convey different messages in different countries;
- photos used in English editions do not always 'translate' to other countries; and
- bold statements used in the UK, such as 'we are the biggest . . . the best . . .' are not always esteemed in other cultures.

These lists are by no means exhaustive but they do illustrate how the production of a quality end product involves collaboration between various experts and a great deal of detailed planning.

PRIORITIES AND DEADLINES

Why cut the 'Quality' cloth?

Perhaps in reading this far you have come to the conclusion that this all sounds far too convoluted and painstaking. If you do, I have to say that I disagree!

I say this not only because I am a linguist but also, and more importantly, because:

- I believe in the broad concepts of 'Total Quality';
- I have seen the end results of not adhering to the principles of 'Quality';
- I have seen the delight of overseas agents and customers when they *do* 'read what they want to read'; and
- if you believe that your product, service or organisation are worthy of the attention of the outside world then you might as well do things properly.

'Mr Reasonable'

'Mr Reasonable' is the organisation or individual who, having signed on to these principles then also acts upon them. Nobody really enjoys working under massive pressure unless it is for isolated and meaningful reasons with a targeted end result. This also applies to translators, copywriters, proofreaders and printers, all of whom can deliver the right product when they deal with 'Mr Reasonable'.

In turn, 'Mr Reasonable' has an insight into the stages and processes involved in this 'Quality' process.

CAN COMPUTERS HELP?

Maximise their potential

Computers and information technology have increasingly important roles to play. For example:

- a text which undergoes all of the stages referred to above can be passed from stage to stage on disc; continued retyping and the puzzled head-scratching over illegible alterations need not always apply;
- if you 'sort out' the technology in advance with your printer, it is feasible for the disc which contains your final text to be converted much more rapidly to top quality printing;

- the emergence of desk top publishing and the increasing sophistication of the available packages make DTP an ideal vehicle for certain publications; and
- storage of texts for amended reprints is greatly facilitated by information technology. In addition, translators can develop glossaries and vocabulary lists of specialist terms.

Limitations

The day is not yet here when machines can fulfil all of your translation requirements. Undoubtedly, great strides will be made in the years to come. By and large, computers *can* translate, for example, lists of instructions which involve simple commands ('insert the . . ., connect the . . ., switch on the . . .'). Indeed, computer user manuals are often translated in this way.

Texts which involve cultural adaptation and a more colourful use of language (persuasion, recommendation, detail, etc.) are not really yet capable of being machine-translated.

Finally, some do's and don'ts:

don't
- leave it too late;
- put everybody involved under pressure;
- regard the process as simply 'translation' . . . or even 'printing';
- disregard the expert views of those involved; and
- forget your 'Quality' objectives;

do
- give it plenty of time;
- involve and consult the relevant experts;
- ensure that checking procedures are available; and
- enjoy the positive benefits of providing your first class product, service or organisation with 'first class' support.

CHAPTER THIRTEEN

LANGUAGES FOR THE SMALL/MEDIUM-SIZED BUSINESS

KEITH ROBINSON

CAN A LANGUAGE STRATEGY WORK FOR A SMALL BUSINESS?

• Defining the problem • What is a small business? • Why bother with language issues? • What might Smallco's language objectives be?

THE IMPORTANCE AND COSTS OF A LANGUAGE STRATEGY

• Without a language strategy what could go wrong? • Cost versus benefit • Elements of the strategy • Making it pay

WHAT SHOULD IT INCLUDE?

• The broad strategy • Setting realistic objectives • Planning ahead

WILL IT REALLY MAKE ANY DIFFERENCE?

• Key questions • Building the bridge • Checklist for action • The payback

> The year: 2000. Smallco Ltd, a small local company, has successfully extended its market to include two countries in Continental Europe and is now planning to extend its

activities into a third country. Its employees are convinced that languages play a fundamental role in the growth of the business, and recognise the advantages this gives the company over its competitors. They believe that the firm's language strategy now makes a significant contribution to the growth of the company.

Links have been made with providers of language services who can respond quickly to the language needs of the organisation. Customers appreciate the benefits of communications in their own language and employees have been stimulated by the contact with customers in mainland Europe to improve their own language skills. Sales and technical literature in their own language is greatly appreciated by customers. The international flavour to daily business life has brought a new dimension to the people involved who are highly motivated by the feeling of belonging to a progressive organisation. The stimulus of the international dimension has produced ideas for new markets which have substantially increased the *profitability* of the company.

CAN A LANGUAGE STRATEGY WORK FOR A SMALL BUSINESS?

Defining the problem

To many people the Smallco scenario seems an impossible dream. Small companies suffer all the problems of attitude to language of big companies, except more so. Most small companies have not even realised there is a problem, let alone arrived at a solution.

And yet is a small business any different from a multinational except in its size? It still has customers who need to be satisfied, staff who need to be motivated and managers who must be committed. Like the multinational, it faces the problem of communication. Sales staff must communicate with production people and both must communicate with the administrators and financial people. All of them must communicate with customers and suppliers. The need for good communication is of paramount importance to any business regardless of its size.

What is a small business?

So how important is its size? Depending on whom you consult, a small business could be anything from a one-man band to an organisation employing 500 people. In deciding from a language point of view whether the business is small, it is not the number of people in the organisation that matters, but whether the business has in-house language professionals. We shall consider in this chapter how a small business, defined as one which does not have in-house language professionals, can achieve its language objectives.

Why bother with language issues?

Small businesses have tended to operate in local markets. Generally speaking, the smaller the business the less its owners are aware of the world around it.

The Single Market is changing all that. Legislation is being published every day which fundamentally affects small business. To imagine that the Single Market does not affect you because you do not export is to delude yourself. European Community legislation is putting people out of business simply because they are not aware that it exists.

One small UK company producing a distinctive product unavailable in the EC countries of mainland Europe discovered that EC legislation covering standards in its industry did not contain reference to its product. Had it not been in touch with developments in Europe it would have been unable to produce its main product and therefore would have been legislated out of existence. Because it was aware of the importance of European legislation it lobbied the European Community with the effect that a description of its main product was incorporated into the appropriate European legislation. Not only did this enable it to continue supplying its home market, but it gave the company a significant advantage had it wished to enter export markets since the specification of its main product was enshrined in the appropriate European directive.

The more a business becomes aware of market opportunities in Europe and beyond, the more it is faced with recognising and solving the language problem. It has to devise and implement a strategy for dealing with language and cultural issues.

What might Smallco's language objectives be?

A language strategy is a cornerstone of international business. Any business, small or large, which wishes to operate in international markets will fail without a language strategy. Smallco must decide what its trading objectives are, and devise its language strategy to help achieve them.

Smallco must set achievable language objectives. It cannot expect its people to become fluent speakers of a multitude of languages or efficient translators of technical manuals and publicity material. Smallco must, however, decide what language objectives it needs to achieve to make the most significant impact on the success of its business. These might include:

• improved communication with foreign customers and suppliers; and
• improved language awareness among its own staff.

Improving communication with overseas customers and suppliers by writing letters, promotional material and technical manuals in their own language will fundamentally alter their approach to the company. The impact on your foreign colleague of providing him with complete information in his own language cannot be underestimated. If your staff can at least introduce themselves in the language of the customer then the impact is greater still. Smallco should not be overawed by the magnitude of the language task but should identify those areas within its business where an improvement in language skills would bring the most benefit.

Addressing the language issues in those areas will form the foundation of its language strategy. Once this investment is seen to produce a pay-off, Smallco may identify additional language needs which can be addressed at a later stage.

The elements within a language strategy for Smallco may initially be few in number but with the right professional help there is no reason why an effective language strategy cannot be implemented.

THE IMPORTANCE AND COST OF A LANGUAGE STRATEGY

Without a language strategy what could go wrong?

Language issues are little understood by small firms. Even when language needs are recognised, they are usually met (after a fashion!) in an unprofessional way using people with limited language ability.

The language interface is so often the weak link in the chain.

There are numerous examples of costly promotional literature failing to achieve its objective because of poor translation. The problem is that the small business very rarely becomes aware of the real reason for these failures. It does not understand the importance of having access to high quality language skills. When sales do not materialise it may be assumed that its market intelligence was incorrect and the market does not exist. The fault, however, may lie not with its product but in the way in which it is presented.

Cost versus benefit

I recently saw in a business to business journal an advertisement by a German company seeking a UK distributor. It read: 'German company selling unmatched hinges seeks UK distributor.' The image of a door with three non-matching hinges is amusing but is unlikely to produce for that German company the UK distributor it is seeking. Indeed, the impression given is that an organisation which produces written material of such poor quality cannot be worth dealing with.

A translation such as this may not cost much but nor will it bring any benefit. The small business is preoccupied with minimising cost, especially when it involves buying in expert consultancy services in areas which it does not understand. Nowhere more so than in language services which neither the business nor its advisors regard as important. Educating small businesses in the importance of language is a long-term process aimed at encouraging them to appreciate the value of high quality language skills. If that process is successful, small businesses will begin to allocate time to the language issue.

The small business which is committed to a language strategy may have one great advantage over its large competitors. Adapting the diagrams on pages 4 and 5 for the small business could produce something like this:

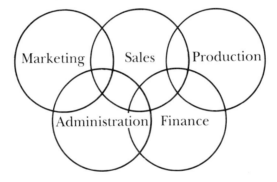

The interfaces or overlap areas are the same:

But it may be easier for a language strategy to penetrate these interfaces in a small business than in a large one. In the case of a small business, all these functions may be carried out or at least controlled by one individual. Convincing that person of the importance of the strategy will make them realise the impact that it could have throughout their business. No-one comes up with more ideas than a highly motivated small business owner. Certainly once it is convinced of the need for a language strategy the small business will be in a position to implement it much more quickly than a large organisation.

Elements of the strategy

A language strategy for a small business will differ from that of a large company in that it will rely to a large extent on the bought-in services of full-time language professionals.

The main services the small company will require are:

- translation of documents and correspondence;
- the production of promotional literature in foreign languages;
- language training;
- business culture training; and
- interpreting.

It may also require assistance in determining what its language needs are (i.e. a 'language audit' – see chapter 2).

Making it pay

In its simplest form, the cost of a language strategy is the cost of paying language professionals for their services. Without incurring these costs, Smallco could not do the business. The costs of implementing its language strategy are negligible by comparison with the research and development, marketing and selling costs which would be wasted if it did not have the means of communicating effectively with its customers.

- The implementation of a language strategy will only succeed in the small firm if those at the top of the organisation understand its importance and are totally committed to its implementation.
- To summarise, the language strategy for a small business must be relevant, profit-generating and cost-effective.

WHAT SHOULD IT INCLUDE?

The broad strategy

We said earlier that the benefits to Smallco of a language strategy would be:

- improved communication with foreign customers and suppliers; and
- improved language awareness among its own staff.

> A foreigner came to England and set up as a barrowboy in the East End of London. An Englishman bought from him regularly and was impressed by his command of English. Some years later the Englishman was on a sales trip in a foreign country and was surprised to find that the buyer was his old friend from the East End. He began his sales pitch in English but the foreigner stopped him and asked that the discussion should be conducted in his own language. The Englishman asked why this should be. 'I know you speak fluent English. I used to buy from you in London,' he said. 'Ah yes,' said the foreigner, 'but then I was *selling*'.

The mistake made by many small firms is to assume that to buy dictionaries and to give staff a little language training will solve the problem. It will not. Smallco cannot rely on its own personnel to solve its language problems. Smallco staff already have a full-time job dealing with their normal business activities. Not only can they not be spared to do additional work but since they are not skilled in language they do not have the necessary expertise. No amount of language training and guidance will enable Smallco's employees to become skilled translators and interpreters. *This role must be left to the professionals.*

> An unskilled interpreter was obviously responsible for one of my favorite language howlers. The English proverb 'Out of sight, out of mind' was translated into the foreign language equivalent of 'invisible idiot'!

Setting realistic objectives

Smallco must set itself realistic language objectives. Referring back to the diagram earlier in the chapter, it must define the interfaces where language skills are most important. Internal or bought-in language skills must be used to fill the gaps. Smallco is unlikely to have adequate language skills in-house and must seek to meet its language needs from elsewhere.

Establishing close links with full-time language professionals who can provide translating and interpreting services is a good first step. Such organisations can produce promotional literature in the customer's own language and translate letters between Smallco and its customer abroad. This seems elementary, yet very few small businesses think of attempting to have literature, and particularly correspondence, professionally translated into the foreign language.

Even if Smallco *has* some in-house language ability, it must still consider to what extent it can cope with responses from its overseas contacts in their own language. There is little point in Smallco holding itself out as having high-grade language skills if the first letter or telephone call from abroad is misunderstood or, worse still, ignored.

It might be wise to tell the foreign customer that the language skills of the company are limited and that it is for this reason that the letter has been professionally translated into the foreign language. Smallco should also mention that the company has access to the services of interpreters should the need arise. At least in this way the foreign customer will be impressed that Smallco has made the effort, yet aware that its language skills are limited.

Once it has established links with outside language professionals, Smallco can seek to improve the language skills among its own staff. Even in small companies there are often individuals who have some interest or experience in languages.

It cannot do the firm any harm to encourage those people to develop their skills further through:

• training;
• personal tuition; and
• business culture training.

It is vital for the small business to understand that a language strategy is not an option but a necessity in doing international business.

Planning ahead

After long negotiations, the terms have been agreed with the German customer and an agreement has been drafted in English. The Managing Director of Smallco is to go to Germany tomorrow to sign the contract. Suddenly he realises that he does not have a copy of the agreement in German. He telephones his professional translator and asks her to produce a translation by the following morning.

This happens all too often. Conveying meaning in another language is not simply a matter of referring to dictionaries. Translators cannot possibly produce a quality professional job in an unrealistic time scale. Their job is not simply to translate the English words into German but also to review the document in a German context. They will need background information to enable them to undertake the translation and will need to review and discuss the translation and resulting queries with the company. They may wish to consult legal experts, possibly in Germany. If Smallco gives them less than 24 hours in which to do the work the translators cannot possibly do the job justice. They must either produce a job of less than perfect quality (which professionally they should not do) or fail to deliver in time which will damage (unfairly) their reputation with their client.

An interpreter, too, will need background information before the meeting. He or she will also need you to conduct the discussion in short segments with breaks during which the interpreting can be performed.

By thinking language at an earlier stage, Smallco will be able to involve its language professionals at the right time. The resulting quality documentation and professional presentations will enhance its quality image.

WILL IT REALLY MAKE ANY DIFFERENCE?

Key questions

- What would your reaction be to receiving promotional litera-ture from a foreign company which is not translated into English?
- How would you react to a legal agreement translated into a form of English which neither you nor your lawyers could understand?
- What if you cannot understand the language of the after-sales staff who are supposed to help you?

Building the bridge

Can we really expect a positive response unless we at least go some way towards convincing our customer that we are attempting to break the language barrier?

> I remember some years ago being in Sweden. I spoke no Swedish at all but needed to find a Post Office. How embarrassing it was to stop people in the street and speak to them in what to them was a foreign language! Just a few words would have made all the difference!

Smallco cannot afford to be in this position. It is developing a language strategy because it needs one. It saw opportunities to develop into overseas markets and has made a positive decision to explore them. An overseas market is different from the home market not only because the customers speak a different lan-guage; they also have different laws, customs and business etiquette. Smallco understands that to approach foreign markets without at least a broad understanding of the cutlural differences is a recipe for disaster (see chapter 10).

A language strategy is not an objective in itself; it is only a means to an end. That end is the expansion of the business into new markets.

Checklist for action

The language strategy affects all aspects of Smallco's business. It affects research, development, production, promotion, marketing and advertising whether these functions are carried out by its own personnel or by external advisors. By controlling the impact of language in its business, Smallco:

- ensures that its staff think of the language issues at an early stage;
- involves its suppliers and sub-contractors in planning language issues;
- plans and budgets for language costs;
- uses only language professionals;
- ensures that they are briefed comprehensively and in time;
- uses technical translators when appropriate;
- requires its language professionals to exercise quality control over technical translators; and
- ensures that all technical translations are checked by a native speaker of the language into which they have been translated.

The payback

Smallco sees a language strategy as a fundamental part of its way of doing business and not as an unbudgeted add-on cost. Smallco's staff seek to apply the same quality standards to dealings with foreign customers as they apply to those with customers in the home market. They do not have the language expertise themselves and therefore must buy it in from professional experts. Before they visit overseas customers they are briefed by experts on the differences in behaviour and ways of doing business between their own country and that of their customer. They found that once they began to visit overseas markets their confidence increased dramatically. This has encouraged them to take advantage of subsidised trade missions organised by government, development organisations and local authorities. Smallco's personnel have found that the greatest spur to learning a foreign language is to visit the country and to feel helpless! They realise that they may never be competent to negotiate business deals in a foreign language but they have experienced at first hand the dramatic change in attitude on the part of their foreign colleagues when they speak to them in their own language.

Encouraged by the success of its language strategy to date, Smallco is looking forward to entering new overseas markets. Its staff are gaining in confidence both as a result of improvement in their own language expertise and through the good impression created on its customers by the quality service provided by its external language professionals.

From its customers Smallco has received the ultimate accolade. They do not think of it as a foreign supplier. The material they receive is accurately translated into their own language and their communications with the company are always promptly and professionally dealt with. The implementation of its language strategy enables Smallco to project in an international marketplace the same quality standards it has always practised at home. The result is predictable. The customers keep coming back for more!

CHAPTER FOURTEEN

IN-COMPANY LANGUAGE TRAINING

Three Case Studies

DOUG EMBLETON, HELEN HANCY & HEIDI GANNON

ICI CHEMICALS AND POLYMERS
- How did it all start? • What is provided?

NORWICH UNION
- How did it all start? • What is provided?

LLOYD'S OF LONDON
- How did it all start? • What is provided?

SIMILARITIES AND CONVERGING FACTORS

At this stage in the book it is useful to take a practical look inside three in-company language training systems: ICI Chemicals and Polymers Ltd, Norwich Union and Lloyd's of London. In some senses they are different because they have been developed within the individual structures and cultures of three very different organisations. In other senses, these three systems exhibit similarities because they all share the common objective of providing language training to staff within their respective organisations.

These case studies are certainly not presented as cast-iron principles or guidelines. Indeed, we will see that they are in a constant state of development. The important thing is that they represent three organisations which have made a positive start. Solutions and approaches may well prove to be different for your own organisation but the 'hands on' experience of people who have already started can only be of benefit.

The language training in ICI Chemicals and Polymers forms part of an integrated language strategy which has been constantly adapted and developed over a long period of time and which involves all of the language services covered in the earlier chapter on that subject (translations, interpreting, foreign language publicity, language training). Language training itself has been developed over a period of 20 years and is now provided to over 1200 individuals per year within the organisation. The language training systems in Norwich Union and Lloyd's were initiated much more recently with a conscious focus on the challenges of the Single Market. Thus, whereas the language training in ICI Chemicals and Polymers was the final piece in the integrated language strategy jigsaw the other two systems used language training as the launching pad. The Norwich Union system is gradually moving towards becoming an integrated language strategy whereas the Lloyd's system is essentially based on language training.

ICI CHEMICALS AND POLYMERS

This section will deal solely with the language training operations of ICI Chemicals and Polymers at its Wilton location (near Middlesbrough, Cleveland) although several other language training programmes are operated at other locations within the organisation.

How did it all start?

The early 1970s – before '1992 and all that'
In the early 1970s, the Translations Unit at Wilton changed its

name to the Languages Unit. Hitherto, it had been involved with translations into English, the production of foreign language promotional/product literature and interpreting. The early stages of language training coincided with this change in name and were the principal reason behind the change. Indeed, the inclusion of language training within the portfolio of the Unit's services was a major breakthrough in the development of the concepts of an integrated language strategy. By this time, I had devised, written and taught two German audio-visual courses for engineers for one of the Company's graduate recruitment schemes and the idea of organising language training for our full-time staff was appealing.

The first language audit

An approach was made to the Training Department who agreed to organise a language needs questionnaire. This is what we nowadays call a language audit. The results revealed a high level of job-related interest in on-site language training and a small number of weekly classes were arranged in French and German. At the very start, I was involved in teaching one of the German classes.

The first group classes

Classes were based on an academic year and had the 'end-of-year' objective of an independent, external examination (which was not and never has been compulsory). We opted for an examining body which would conduct the examinations on our own premises and for an examination procedure which adequately tested our candidates but which did not excessively intrude on their already busy schedules.

The classes were held at a rate of two hours per week at set times. Looking back on those early days several key issues spring to mind:

* finding suitable teachers and materials was not easy;
* the lack of a permanent 'base' for the classes involved a great deal of administration work as did the organising of examinations, class registers, and communications with students and teachers; and of course

- towards the end of the first 'academic year' we were already heavily engaged in organising the next academic year.

Ever since we started in the early 1970s the ball has just kept on rolling and gathering pace. In those early years we cut our teeth and built up our experience. Remember, '1992' had not yet been invented! There were no initiatives, conferences, consciousness-raising coverage of the issues or other stimuli which abound today.

Continuous development

From then until now we have carried on with our learning and developing. In truth, it never stops! We became more involved with in-house individual tuition, arranging residential courses, business culture training, EFL (English as a Foreign Language), the 'Quality' issue, overseas postings, joint ventures, language audits – to name but a few. As our range of services grew, so did the number of users and our networks of contacts and teachers. Eventually, we also found a permanent home for our classes and other training within the Languages Unit. The embodiment of an integrated language service.

In the first year of language training at Wilton we provided four classes to a total of 40 people. Nowadays, tutor-based language training (weekly group classes, in-house one-to-one tuition and crash courses) are provided to a combined total of 1200 people per year at the major UK locations of the organisation.

Resources

It more often than not comes as a great surprise to people when we explain how the Languages Unit is staffed and resourced! There are four full-time staff: the Languages Unit Manager, two graduate linguists (one at Wilton and one at Runcorn) whose main duties are in the translation-based elements of our service and a Personal Assistant. In addition, our most experienced part-time teacher operates in the dual role of part-time Language Training Officer.

In order to efficiently deliver all of the individual language services we therefore rely upon established, tried and trusted networks of suppliers. For example, at Wilton we have a team of over 30 part-time teachers.

What is provided?

Types of training

From our Languages Unit at Wilton we provide:

Weekly classes in a range of languages, still at a rate of two hours per week and on an academic-year basis. London Chamber of Commerce and Industry (LCCI) examinations are held annually on-site and the various class levels equate, both in name and objectives, to the range of LCCI examination levels. All resulting qualifications are entered on the organisation's Personnel Training Records Database.

Individual (one-to-one) tuition is provided in a wide range of languages and situations. There are many situations where the student has a requirement to acquire language skills at a more rapid pace than that afforded by the weekly classes. In terms of flexibility, once the 'introduction' has been made, teacher and student can meet as often and as flexibly as suits.

Residential courses are arranged for many members of staff. We work closely with our external providers and are moving towards the use of a 'common currency' of training outcomes and objectives based on the examination levels. A typical scenario is that we provide on-site individual tuition before, during and after the block of residential weeks. We also liaise closely with the external provider of the residential course to ensure that there is continuity between our work and their work with the student.

Costings and resources

Our language training now operates as a 'cost centre' and we use internal accounting mechanisms to charge per capita fees for group classes and hourly rates for individual tuition. User departments also pay the costs of residential courses. This 'pay as you go' system is an acid test of the need for good on-site language training. Demand continues to escalate and internal customers would therefore appear to be happy with what they are paying for.

Our teachers work on a part-time basis within the terms of a prescribed, annually renewable contract for part-time work. 'Quality' training and staff development are infinitely more complicated when they involve part-time staff but we do hold teacher meetings and workshops and we have a regular newsletter. Undoubtedly, the fact that language training and the Languages Unit have a *permanent* base is vital. At least we see our teachers on every visit; they feel that they provide training at an identifiable venue; materials and equipment are on hand; we can exercise 'walking the floor' management and monitoring of the training – and, therefore, the whole programme assumes some sort of 'team identity'.

The need for a finger on the pulse

After a few years of building up some experience in in-company language training, we devised the post of Language Training Officer. This remains today a part-time post but is a vital part of the training programme. The Language Training Officer not only works in the capacity of a part-time teacher (and therefore delivers some of the language training), but also acts as the link between the Languages Unit Manager and the training programme. It is fundamentally important that somebody has their finger on the pulse at all times and that this person also participates in the training process. For example, one must be able to monitor:

- how different teachers are performing;
- any potential friction within classes or groups (the 'false beginner' who would shine in – and therefore disrupt – a beginners' class is a classic case);
- how different materials are being received by the students;
- suggestions for improvement to the programme – these may come at any time from any person, teacher or student (as with any successful suggestion scheme, the suggester has to know how and with whom to suggest); and
- how new developments (e.g. use of video) are proceeding.

Spreading the word

As a small business within a very large business we need to advertise and promote our services. For example, during the pre-academic-year enrolment period we will arrange for articles in works newspapers and posters on all notice boards; several 'Advice Days' will be held to enable students to talk about their needs and appropriate training in detail; information packs will be sent to all enquirers. These will contain details of timetables, costs, examination levels (and definitions of the skills which these entail) and a detachable enrolment form.

Facts and figures

- In-house weekly group classes are charged back to users on a per capita fee basis. The fee covers 38 weeks (76 hours of tuition), the coursebook and end-of-year examination fee.
- A total of over 60 weekly classes are provided in the North-East and North-West (Wilton, Billingham and Runcorn).
- Classes tend to be made up of people from a wide range of departments and functions.
- Language training for career and personal development now comes very high on the agenda of younger members of staff.
- LCCI examinations are held on-site towards the end of each academic year. The examination levels are also used to define class titles and levels and student ability ranges. Examinations are optional and at the last Wilton session, just over 100 students successfully completed LCCI examinations.
- The 'menu' of language training services is:
  - weekly group classes;
  - special classes for common interest groups;
  - on-site one-to-one tuition;
  - EFL tuition;
  - language audits for individual departments or sites;
  - language needs analyses for individuals (in order to devise a tailor-made training package); and
  - off-site, residential crash courses.
- The main languages taught are German, French, Spanish, Italian, Dutch, Japanese and English. In a typical year we will also arrange tuition in, for example, Chinese, Thai, Portuguese, Russian and Arabic.

As the service has developed we have become involved in EFL (English language training) for overseas colleagues and their families and also in business culture training. Above all, the initial consultation between our Unit and the individual is vital and enables us to devise training programmes to match individual needs.

The Languages Unit still provides all of the other specialist services within an integrated language strategy. As a result, it has become a clearly identifiable centre of language expertise.

Finally, some typical language training scenarios which illustrate just a few of the situations which we handle.

Fred 'X' and his family are to be posted to France for three years on a special project. The initial consultation concentrates upon things such as: his language learning track record, his job objectives and role in France, his time availability, and requirements of other family members. This will lead to firm proposals on training programmes (combining in-house individual tuition and residential tuition) which will include time required, methods, materials and costs.

Mary 'Y' is working on market development of her product in Germany. She has 'A' Level German but recent forays into Germany have revealed.some specific needs. The initial consultation will focus upon those specific needs and will lead to firm proposals on in-house individual tuition, self-study 'back-up' materials and residential business culture and presentation skills training (in German).

Family 'B' has arrived from Japan and the husband will be working with us in the UK for two years. Initial consultation will focus upon: his training needs and objectives, time availability, and the needs of other family members. As a result, specialist EFL (English) teachers will be used. The teacher(s) used for the family members will also be skilled in cultural integration and in the specific learning needs of very young children. At the end of the overseas posting, an on-site examination will be arranged which will have great relevance to the husband's Japanese managers on his return to Japan and will be totally valid for inclusion in his personnel record in Japan.

It has been possible only to scratch the surface in this case study but hopefully I have shown what can be achieved via a long-term approach to in-house language training.

What are the benefits to the organisation and to individuals? Too numerous to mention in full, but to name a few:

- the language training is accessible, 'on tap', and flexible;
- we collect dozens of tales every year of 'how my language came in *really* useful'; and
- the training is part of a totally professional and integrated approach (since we also provide translations, interpreting, language audits and foreign language publicity).

And for me personally:

- the sound of laughter and enjoyment from a classroom from people who are at the start, in the middle or at the end of a very busy day, is an indication that we have got things into perspective!

NORWICH UNION

In contrast to ICI, the Language Unit at Norwich Union is still very much in its infancy. Under its integrated language strategy, the Language Unit coordinates language training, translating and all other language services required by the Group, such as proof-reading, text-scanning or consultancy. These services are concentrated at our Head Office in Norwich, but we try where possible to assist the branch network and overseas offices as well. In the context of this chapter, I have limited my coverage to language training activities.

How did it all start?

Opportunities and the Single Market

The decision to create an in-house Language Unit at Norwich Union was not taken lightly. The original idea of researching language training options was initiated in 1988 by a small team of staff with a brief to examine opportunities in Europe in the light of the Single European Market, and was investigated as a joint venture with our Training School, combining expertise in:

- language skills;
- *adult* training; and
- the company: its structure, procedures and policies.

I recall vividly my horror at discovering how little the majority of my colleagues understood of foreign languages. All of the fallacies and misconceptions mentioned earlier in this book were in evidence to some degree, and it was not easy to convince the sceptics (who will always exist) of why language training was needed and what was required.

Reviewing the options

Our investigations covered a wide range of options; we talked to local training providers, including further education establishments, private language companies, agencies and private individuals, and we also visited the Languages Units at ICI and Peugeot Talbot for help and advice. This enabled us to compare options in terms of:

- price;
- quality of the tuition;
- administration;
- flexibility (e.g. times of day and times of year available);
- premises;
- our ability to influence the training programme; and
- ways of monitoring training.

Further studies were undertaken to determine the scale and nature of demand (i.e. a language audit), and the results were then compared with the solution available. On this basis, our final recommendation was that for Norwich Union an integrated in-house service would best suit requirements. Finally, the implementation of such a scheme was broken down into practical steps, including costings. Eighteen months after setting out, the company finally approved our proposals, and the Language Unit at Norwich Union was born.

Unusually perhaps, the new Unit was located within the European Division, as it was felt that there was a natural link between the two areas. For many companies, it might seem more natural for language training to become part of an existing in-house training service. At Norwich Union, the Training School is primarily concerned with technical and management skills training; the European Division was already concerned with languages as a part of its work. Since I too already worked there, it seemed a natural choice of location when I was asked to create the Unit.

Selection of teachers

The Unit started life in January 1990 as a team of two; myself as a qualified linguist, plus a young, enthusiastic clerical assistant. The first months were spent in turmoil, with a number of mammoth tasks to be tackled, including recruiting self-employed tutors. This we did by placing a carefully worded advertisement in the local press (our Staff Department helped us to produce the required text). We invited applications from:

- qualified teachers;
- with experience of teaching adults;
- with some commercial experience, where possible in insurance; and
- with excellent language skills (i.e. it was not essential to be a native speaker).

All interviews were conducted by myself as a linguist with teaching experience; applicants were also considered in the light of their personality, e.g. a positive attitude (we were particularly careful to avoid a 'school' situation in our classes).

Choosing materials

We then had to evaluate and select appropriate course materials. Again, as a linguist, I initially reviewed materials available for adults by visiting bookshops, examining catalogues, requesting sample copies and seeking recommendations from other adult trainers. We then invited our tutors to meet and discuss materials (by language), before submitting their recommendations. The Language Unit retained the casting vote, but we managed to agree on a number of 'core' courses. Our selection was based on such criteria as:

- suitability of the course for adults;
- good, lively presentation;
- well-structured chapters and a clear teaching progression;
- a good balance between grammar and conversation;
- relevance of topics covered; and
- availability of back-up materials, e.g. audio/video cassettes, student workbooks, teachers' guide.

We resisted then (and continue to resist) suggestions that we should use cheap 'short-cuts', such as self-tuition packages. We firmly believe that these do not offer a valid alternative to teacher–student contact. It is also important to point out that language courses (and, indeed, languages themselves) are constantly evolving; in fact, new courses appear with a rapidity which rivals the emergence of new software packages. It is therefore essential that someone with linguistic and teaching expertise continues to monitor developments in language teaching (including new training media such as CBT and interactive video), and that changes are implemented where appropriate. We also find it helpful to keep a library of materials, including books, audio and video cassettes, newspapers, even authentic insurance materials in foreign languages, for both tutors and students to use.

Promoting the service

Finally, we set about advertising our classes through:

- individually designed advertisements on in-house notice-boards;
- circulars; and
- articles in the in-house newssheet, etc.

We have found it essential to maintain a relatively high profile ever since, in order to keep interest in language-learning alive.

Our first courses were finally launched in April 1990.

What is provided?

Our audit had revealed a huge interest amongst staff for language training; indeed, demand was such that we chose to launch two parallel programmes.

Sponsored language training

The first, and the most significant in terms of the company's objectives, was sponsored language training. Managers were invited to nominate staff in their area who required language training for their job and the costs of the tuition were then charged to their cost centre. Thus, managers had ultimate control over who was trained.

Originally, 30 staff were nominated; this has since increased to 100 staff learning seven languages (French, German, Spanish, Italian, Dutch, Portuguese and EFL). Tuition is delivered on an individual or paired basis by a tutor selected by the Language Unit on the basis of students' personal needs and objectives, which are established during a preliminary discussion and then recorded in a Training Plan. This provides both tutor and student with tangible training objectives, and allows the Language Unit to monitor their programme with bi-monthly assessments prepared by the tutors, plus a six-monthly review meeting between the student, tutor and a member of the Language Unit. All students on this scheme are encouraged (not forced) to sit commercial examinations, chosen on the same basis as for ICI; these not only offer the student a further incentive, but also provide managers who have funded the training with tangible proof of progress.

> A section leader in an area dealing with overseas claims who already spoke French and Spanish, was sponsored to learn German to help deal with claims from the British Forces in Germany. A year later, she has passed her first examination, and is now preparing for the Intermediate LCCI exam, which will develop her ability to use spoken German in a work-related context.

This scheme is constantly reviewed as it evolves. Feedback on the performance of tutors and students is essential to all schemes; we use the monitoring outlined above, questionnaires and tutor workshops to determine where problems lie. Currently we are tackling such questions as:

- the relatively high cost of individual tuition (although progress is usually faster than in a group);

- the fact that individual tuition provides the tutor and student with limited scope for conversation practice. There is no group interaction as in a class situation, where students can be involved in pairwork, and learn from mistakes made by fellow students. Individual teaching can also be lonely for the student (and at times the tutor), who has no other students with whom to share learning problems and successes. (Solutions have included tutors bringing together individual students on a regular basis, and half-day workshops in a particular target language); and
- the process for selecting students is inadequate; some managers are more positive towards languages than others, and we know of staff with a very real need for training who have been unable to obtain the support of their manager. Hence we are examining ways in which the Language Unit can take a more proactive role in shaping the language strategies of individual departments.

Staff with personal reasons for learning

Our second scheme is aimed at staff who have personal reasons for learning (or who have not succeeded in obtaining sponsorship). Typically, these are staff who have developed an interest in a country and its language from holidays abroad or family connections, and want to be able to converse with natives of that country in their own language.

The same tutors provide group lessons based upon compatible learning levels. The problem of assessing students' levels at the outset is considerable; we do not have the time to interview each applicant on this scheme individually, so we issue a fairly detailed application form asking about previous experience in the language they wish to study (and also in any other languages they have learned). The drawback to this method is that people often under- or overestimate their own ability (either deliberately or otherwise); we have so far avoided assessment tests because of the time taken to administer them and the fact that we feel they would deter a great many potential learners. Instead, we offer newcomers the option of trying a group (or groups) until they find one which they and the tutor feel is appropriate. They pay nothing until they find their level.

Classes are held on-site, but outside of core flex-times (i.e. lunchtimes and after 4.00 pm) using conference/meeting rooms where available (although we have recently been allocated a permanent room, which has helped considerably). Students meet the cost of the tutor themselves, but the company provides the accommodation and administration (which should not be under-estimated!). Student numbers fluctuate on a seasonal basis, and range between 800 and 350.

We currently offer all the languages available for sponsored tuition plus Greek, Japanese and Russian; the basic principle has always been to offer classes in any language or at any level if there is sufficient demand to make it commercially viable (we generally need a minimum of six students, and try not to exceed 10 per group). Again, however, there are still many problems to be addressed:

- premises – finding rooms is a problem; students will not tolerate constant room changes and the lack of basic essentials such as a board (in the past, groups have had to take lessons in the staff canteen after work, vying with the cleaners!);
- the demand for lessons and the pressure on rooms is so great that we are forced to limit lessons to one hour per week in order to cater for everyone – ideally, we would like to extend lessons to $1\frac{1}{2}$ hours per week;
- the administration is very complex: we experience regular problems with students who refuse to pay, drop-out rates and room cancellations; and
- in hindsight, we started on too large a scale and tried too hard to cater to individual requests; we now plan to restrict the courses to a reasonable level.

I have only been able to touch briefly upon some of the many complex issues that concern the Language Unit today, but in conclusion, I think that we have been able, despite persistent problems and frequent setbacks, to grow and develop (we are now a team of five full-time linguists with 45 freelance tutors; I myself teach groups, whilst the other members of the team attend at least one class each as students) with company backing, and have significantly improved the skills and effectiveness of key staff in the organisation, as well as the company's overall awareness of, and tolerance towards, foreign languages and cultures. The Norwich Union has made a valuable commitment to long-term training for the future; already, some of our students are enjoying the benefits of this foresight and I have every confidence that it will continue to pay rich dividends as the company develops its business in Europe. With this commitment, the Language Unit will continue to flourish and to provide increasingly valuable services to staff and customers alike.

LLOYD'S OF LONDON

How did it all start?

Lloyd's of London's language programme is based on in-house language training held in Lloyd's Training Centre in the City although courses are also run off-site within constituent Lloyd's companies. I will focus on the in-house courses as they are the model for those which are run off-site.

First, I should clarify one issue: LLoyd's has no official language policy, partly because it is not one company but a marketplace made up of an ever-changing number of companies and partnerships (around 500), each with its own different requirements. This market is serviced by an organisation called the Corporation of Lloyd's of which the Training Centre is part.

Opportunities and the Single Market

In common with other industrial and commercial organisations, Lloyd's thought languages were a 'good thing' because it wished to move some of its emphasis away from the American market to Europe – 1992 was the tangible 'carrot'.

Towards the end of 1988, a Lloyd's Member promised a sum of money to set up a language laboratory. The Market Training Manager conducted research into labs and I, as a UK graduate linguist (in German), was transferred from another Corporation department to run it. Unfortunately, the money never materialised and the linguist remained in the department on other duties. However, the spark had been lit and the Director of Training and his Training Manager continued their research with the spare-time help of the linguist. By talking to Doug Embleton and CILT (the Centre for Information on Language Teaching) we realised that the way forward was not to buy a roomful of expensive but rarely used machines but by high-quality, face-to-face, small group tuition. As there was no budget, in order to be able to continue it was necessary to *prove* that there was a positive demand (rather than a vague feeling) for language training.

Language audit
In consequence, in the summer of 1989, CILT was appointed to carry out a language audit on a representative sample of the Lloyd's companies. Most importantly the survey *proved* the demand and need for language training. It also revealed the languages in demand – and why – and the optimum tuition times.

Finding teachers
The next step was to look at as many sources for language teachers as possible (beware: once they know that a company is even vaguely interested one is inundated with offers, some of them decidedly dubious!). The three main recruitment criteria were:

• good, lively, experienced and committed teachers of *adults* not using the traditional 'school approach' because it was felt that classes should be as oral and participative as possible;
• reliable teachers with contracts who would not suddenly disappear abroad without trace in mid-course; and
• teachers with experience of language training for industry and commerce.

Need for a finger on the pulse
In January 1990, the German linguist was transferred to full-time language duties. However, it was not financially or philosophically viable to have a full-time coordinator who did not also teach, so in February she was sent on an intensive TEFL (Teaching English as a Foreign Language) course.

It was considered philosophically desirable for the coordinator to teach as it was rightly felt that she would not only have 'hands on' experience within the Lloyd's environment but would also have a finger on the pulse of the language training processes. A TEFL course was chosen because:

- the coordinator was a graduate linguist but had no formal teaching qualifications;
- TEFL teacher training courses can be short and highly intensive and provide immediate assessment of the trainee teacher's performance; and
- the TEFL field has conducted much more research in the field of teaching languages to adults and is deemed to be highly progressive.

Moving towards 'start-up'
Publicity was sent out to the Lloyd's market offering beginners' courses in French, German and Spanish early in 1990.

In March 1990, two different suppliers were chosen: one a language school, the other a college; they were to provide one language each and the in-house language coordinator was to provide the third.

People booked onto the courses and it was decided to start with no designated budget or official policy – the proof of the pudding being in the eating. In April 1990, two French, two German and one Spanish beginners' classes started. They were held in the morning or early evening. Needless to say, as is often the case in adult language classes, there were several 'false beginners'! In fact, in the French class, some had French degrees or had lived in France. Fortunately, we had one experienced 'bomb-proof' teacher. Since then we have expanded and learned a lot, not least to interview everyone before putting them into classes.

What is provided?

The Training Centre does not provide a translation service – this is either done company by company or via the Corporation International Department.

Parameters of the training programme
The basic parameters of the language training programme are:

- prior to being selected for a class each student must attend a five-minute interview with the relevant language teacher to assess his or her level (this also gives the coordinator an opportunity to speak to them about the course in general);

- the languages currently provided are French, German, Spanish and Italian;
- they are taught at all levels;
- the courses comprise 40 hours of face-to-face tuition: one two-hour session per week for 20 weeks;
- we recommend that students spend a minimum of 20 minutes every day on consolidation work outside of the class;
- the course is supported by books, audio and video-cassettes, handouts, written homework to be done outside the training room and more recently, by interactive video (in-house);
- the optimum class size is eight, but varies from six to 10;
- the age range is from 18 to the late 50s;
- the professional range is wide, e.g. telephonists, secretaries, trainees, computer programmers, accountants, PR staff, managers, directors, brokers, underwriters, company secretaries, chairmen and members of the board;
- classes are on-site in the Training Department (although some are off-site either in the City or elsewhere in the South-east);
- the start times are: 8.00, 8.30, 9.00, 10.00, 10.30, 12.30 and 13.00 – there are no classes in the late afternoon (due to Lloyd's business patterns) or evening (which have proved to be less successful);
- classes are run every day, many simultaneously;
- two programmes of courses in a calendar year;
- all levels work towards the *optional* FLIC (Foreign Languages in Industry and Commerce) exams of the LCCI at four levels;
- we teach over 120 people;
- the courses are charged in 'real money' for the market delegates (85%) and the Corporation delegates (15%) are cross-charged via the internal accounting system; and
- long weekend study trips to the relevant countries are also arranged.

For a typical long weekend study trip the maximum number for the group is 12 plus the teacher (who does this on a purely voluntary basis and whose expenses are shared between the students and the Training Centre). The group will fly out on a Thursday night and have dinner with either native friends of the tutor or members of our foreign office. The greater part of the next day will be spent in the foreign office.

For the remainder of the weekend there are pre-arranged tours and theatre trips, one or two meals a day with the tutor's native friends as well as free time. All conversation whether at the office, socially or amongst each other is conducted in the target language. The aim is that the students can put all of their classroom role-plays and experience into practice and survive in the foreign country. They all return with a great sense of achievement, self-confidence and motivation as well as having demonstrably improved their language skills. As with classroom sessions, the weekends are carefully structured and balanced between set work and pleasure. The cost of these trips is not included in the course fee. Students either pay out of their own pocket, share the cost with their company or, more usually, the company pays.

Quality control

Monitoring and quality control are vital and therefore:

- the language coordinator is a permanent participant on one course;
- after each programme, a number of classes are selected and each member is interviewed by the coordinator for at least 20 minutes to assess the quality of the programme;
- the coordinator, the Director or the Market Training Manager sit in on classes; and
- the coordinator also takes every possible opportunity to speak to the students, face-to-face or on the telephone.

The programme has now been running for 18 months and has trebled in size but is still in its embryonic stages. There is so much potential still to be fulfilled!

SIMILARITIES AND CONVERGING FACTORS

These three systems of in-company language training provision are developing in different ways. However, there are some remarkable similarities which should be of interest to any organisation contemplating the route to *successful* in-company language training.

The need to find and then foster good teachers of adults – or good external providers of teachers of adults. There is no correlation whatsoever between native speakers and 'good' or 'best' language teachers. For example, it is often the case that the best teacher for beginners' level classes has English as his or her native tongue and can empathise with the needs of beginners.

There are no hard and fast rules and as with all of the services or providers mentioned in this book there are the 'good, the bad and the awful'. All that we are saying is that non-linguist training managers may immediately assume that the best language teachers are foreign nationals. Some are excellent. Some aren't. Quite simply: the best teachers are the best teachers!

This leads us on neatly to the next point:

The need to monitor the training and keep a finger on the pulse. As we have seen from the three case studies it is vital that the language training coordinator, manager, liaison officer or 'whatever the title' is involved in the training programme by actively participating in part of it. This reinforces the same point which is made in chapter 4 on 'Face-to-face tuition'.

Face-to-face tuition is an optimum foundation for in-company language training in combination with other vehicles. ICI Chemicals and Polymers, Norwich Union and Lloyd's all came to the same conclusion: that their language training programmes would be founded upon face-to-face tuition and consolidated by audio materials, videos, computer-assisted learning, business culture training and crash courses where appropriate. All of these other methods and facilities have a very important role to play. However, none of the case study companies opted for a totally open learning, open access approach to the language training issue.

As we have seen in other chapters, the use of other language training processes and materials (audio materials, TV/video, computer-assisted learning, interactive video, crash courses and business culture training) can be vital ingredients of an overall language training strategy. Indeed, it should be emphasised that a staple diet of two hours per week of face-to-face tuition *must* be consolidated by at least four hours of work by the student away from the classroom. Audio and video materials can be used as part of the classroom tuition and for consolidation work. Computers and interactive video material can be used for consolidation work. Business culture training and crash courses have obvious roles to play where a weekly two-hour diet or the acquisition of language skills alone are not appropriate.

Therefore, open access learning as a means of consolidation and in tandem with face-to-face tuition is highly effective. However, the organisations in the three case studies would not recommend high investment in and *total* reliance on open access learning, no matter how attractive or sophisticated it may seem. It is our experience that the attractions and benefits of 'open access learning' for other management/staff training issues do not apply to language training.

In addition, it is worth noting that the three case study systems are all being managed and developed by *linguists*.

The seemingly less important matters such as accommodation or administration are quite essential to the success of the programme. There are a lot of issues at stake here, including commitment. Managers frequently suffer if their secretary or PA is away for any reason. Good secretaries are the life blood of many systems. This concept applies equally to language training programmes if one stops to consider the need for the 'bare necessities' such as room bookings, registers, communications – written and verbal, incoming and outgoing – with students and teachers, student records, making sure that the right equipment is available for the right class, purchasing materials, preparing progress reports, arranging timetables, organising examinations. The provision of 'Quality' language training is, of course, paramount but any strategy simply has to have these basic foundations.

Independent assessment (by examination) need not be compulsory but is an invaluable measurement tool. Whilst it is inappropriate to deter any adult language learner from pursuing an interest in and a dedication to 'languages' one has to put in-company language training in a business context. It is not always good enough for language training to be a 'good thing' or 'nice to have'. Nor do managers respond well to funding language training programmes or training for individuals when progress is defined subjectively by terms such as 'is doing well' and 'has made a great improvement'.

If it is to succeed in a business context, language training has to reach those individuals who will really benefit and who, as a consequence, will be able to use their language skills as a contribution to their organisation's activities. It is our experience that those students who 'stay the course' also move towards formal qualifications. The two seem to go hand in hand. As Norwich Union has found, it is ultimately more effective to train well those people who *really* need the language than to train whole hosts of people.

In-company language training in the UK is in its infancy, and yet never has the time been more right. Perhaps the key messages are these:

- 'Evolution not revolution'. Don't necessarily be carried away with thoughts of grandiose schemes. Get the foundations right. Get your commitment right. Don't just dip a toe in but don't dive in either. Use the steps at the side of the pool.
- Build upon success. Once your commitment and foundations are in place, review the success stories ... and then do some more building.
- Allow and enable in-company linguists and training providers to be proactive. They just might surprise – and delight you!
- Relate the successes of language training (and indeed, of all language services) to real issues like international markets, international communications, overseas postings, joint ventures and allow these successes to be acknowledged and to become part of the organisation and its culture.
- Don't pay lip service to the '1992' messages – or to linguists – or to language skills. Allow them some room and they will certainly reward you.

CHAPTER FIFTEEN

TQM AND AN INTEGRATED LANGUAGE STRATEGY

Perfect Partners?

DOUG EMBLETON

TOTAL QUALITY MANAGEMENT
• Broad concepts of TQM • TQM as a partner for a language strategy

TQM AND THE LANGUAGE AUDIT
• The transition from 'quick-fix' language services to a TQM approach • Before TQM and the language audit • After TQM and the language audit

PRACTICAL EXAMPLES
• Quality also has a small 'q' • Poor quality costs • Quality distinguishes • Customers welcome it • Staff love it • Competitors are doing it! • Quality is profitable

ENDPIECE

TOTAL QUALITY MANAGEMENT

In chapter 1, I described the concept of an *integrated language strategy* and briefly reviewed the individual components of such a strategy. The ensuing chapters will have provided you with expert and comprehensive information on these individual components. In effect, we have dismantled the whole 'strategy' machine and enabled you to examine its individual working parts in detail.

This final chapter reassembles all of these individual components and establishes the positive and meaningful connections between the integrated language strategy and the realities of the business world. I will attempt a variation on one of my original professional skills by 'translating' the excellence of the specialist information contained in this book to sound, business-driven and undeniable reasons for implementing such a strategy. The formulation and dosage of the strategy have to be defined by the real, business needs of the organisation and the selection of the most appropriate combination of the components described in this book.

Broad concepts of TQM

As my 'dictionary' I will use some of the broad concepts of TQM. Other 'reference works' which I will use for this translation will include human resource development, personnel policy, customer service, PR and advertising, long-termism versus short-termism in penetrating overseas markets, joint ventures and acquisitions, and profitability. These references can be altered to match the needs of your particular business or organisation.

It is not my intention to describe in detail the principles of 'Quality' or of 'Total Quality Management' but it will be useful at this stage to list some of the very broad concepts of Quality which have induced me to make the link between TQM and an integrated language strategy. In other words, I believe that in international business TQM and a language strategy cannot possibly do without one another.

I hope that experts in Quality will forgive my perhaps oversimplified view of the topic! On the other hand, since the objective of this book is to demystify the specialist area of language services it is appropriate to apply an equally nuts-and-bolts view of Quality when marrying these two specialist areas.

The broad concepts of Quality – or of TQM – on which this chapter is based are:

- the ultimate beneficiaries of a Quality approach are your organisation's customers;
- as a result of this, your own staff are motivated by being parties to Quality processes and methods and your organisation's efficiency, image – and profits – are enhanced;
- 'getting things right' *costs* – but the cost is justified by the end result;
- 'getting or doing things wrong' *also costs* – there is the cost of doing them in the first place and there is the cost of getting things wrong – lost sales, poor image, having to do it again; and
- Quality is about conforming to requirements. As we can see, there is a price to be paid for conforming to requirements but there is also a huge payback. Equally, there is a price to be paid for not conforming to requirements but this has no payback whatsoever.

TQM as a partner for a language strategy

Total Quality Management is a very convenient dictionary because it is a current and vitally important issue and is therefore almost a management Esperanto. Perhaps more pertinently, the very concept of TQM embraces an organisation and its activities in their entirety. TQM will, by its very nature, include the areas which I have described as reference works. TQM will include all of the relevant areas or functions of *your* business or organisation. Space has limited me to selective examples but I believe that you can apply the same logic to functions in your own organisation or job. Therefore . . .

$$TQM \equiv \text{the totally integrated language strategy}$$

and . . .

<table>
<tr>
<td>

- HRD
- Personnel policy
- Customer service
- PR & advertising
- Long-termism

≡ *Components of TQM*

</td>
<td>

- Language audit
- Translating
- Publicity
- Language training
- Business culture training

≡ *Components of an integrated language strategy*

</td>
</tr>
</table>

In other words, an integrated language policy and an integrated TQM policy are inextricably – and, in the case of international business – unavoidably linked. Having integrated the individual components of a language strategy we can now further integrate them with TQM and the whole organisation.

Several broad areas of TQM can be matched perfectly with the broad areas of a language strategy. I will use the following:

- Quality also has a small 'q'!
- Quality is profitable.
- Poor quality costs.
- Quality distinguishes.
- Customers welcome it.
- Staff love it.
- Competitors are doing it!

TQM AND THE LANGUAGE AUDIT

First, we make a brief return visit to that by now well-known bastion of TQM and good language practice, Carruthers & Co. In chapter 1 we saw that Carruthers & Co. had instigated a language audit in 1993 and that by the year 2000 they were enjoying all of the positive benefits of an integrated language strategy. Let us take another look inside Carruthers & Co. How did they ever get to the language audit stage?

The transition from 'quick-fix' language services to a TQM approach

The year 1993.   Our friends in Carruthers & Co. are fully committed to implanting TQM systems across the whole organisation. Previous Quality exercises in the company have been relatively successful but have tended to concentrate upon the quality of products and specifications. The TQM concept has opened the door to detailed scrutiny of all of the company's functions and activities.

At this stage, Carruthers & Co. have decided to predict how customers and employees would, in fact, recognise a TQM approach within an integrated language strategy and also how things would be different in five years' time. A sticking plaster can save the day. A strategy takes a long time!

They recognise that although they are handling language issues to some extent (for example, the training centres have recently acquired a lot of language learning materials, several people have attended crash courses arranged by their own departments, two of their UK sales offices have independently set up lunchtime French conversation classes, individual members of staff are consistently raising 'languages' as an issue in their annual appraisal interviews, overseas offices are increasingly being called upon – albeit in an uncoordinated way – to advise on foreign language publicity material, a recent bid for a contract has required urgent and accurate translations into Algerian French), they have not reached the stage of 'owning' or defining a policy on foreign language issues. Indeed, no single person in the organisation knows that all of these activities are currently taking place!

The TQM exercise has offered the perfect vehicle for shifting – indeed, for completely reversing – existing angles of perception of language requirements and of how to meet them. As we can see, Carruthers & Co. are already engaged in a wide range of individual but uncoordinated language activities. These are either born of urgent necessity (the quick-fix approach) or via the 'local hero' scenario whereby one person has the initiative to get things going on a small but localised scale. The language audit, under the commitment of the TQM banner, will reveal to a somewhat surprised Carruthers & Co. just how much they are doing already. In effect, Carruthers & Co. will be able to superimpose the concepts of TQM on the concepts of a language strategy. The language strategy will now begin to appeal to the MD, his managers . . . and to the accountants!

In opting for a language audit as the starting point, Carruthers & Co. have been able to use TQM as the source of a genuine commitment to the process. In asking themselves to predict the perceived benefits both to customers and employees of an integrated language strategy in a TQM environment they have also been able to completely reverse introspective and thus totally restrictive angles of perception (such as 'we enter the mystical area of language services only when and if we have to – or because a few people think that we should') to a much more open and positive view of the issues.

TQM and the language audit will enable Carruthers & Co. to look at the opposite end of the equation.

Before TQM and the language audit

Before 1993, before TQM and before the language audit if anybody had asked the management of Carruthers & Co. what the organisation's current language activities were or what the perceived benefits were they would have received the following typical responses. As we can see, the responses are very varied and uncoordinated.

What are our current language activities?
Range of possible responses from key individuals as opposed to a corporate response:

- 'In total, we just don't know.'
- 'As individual activities, currently uncoordinated, they are, as far as we know: Language classes; crash courses; translations; publicity; learning materials in open learning centres.'

What are the perceived benefits?
Range of possible responses:

- 'They're damned expensive.'
- 'I don't know.'
- 'I *think* that we need those activities, but I'm not sure.'
- 'They're an intrusive nuisance.'
- 'If it hadn't been for that excellent translation, we would not have won the contract.'

After TQM and the language audit

In 1993, the combined forces of TQM and the language audit create a totally new approach to the issue.

- Carruthers & Co. accept that within a TQM system:
  - poor quality costs;
  - quality distinguishes;
  - customers welcome it;
  - staff love it; and
  - competitors are doing it!
- Their commitment to broad TQM principles focuses their attitude to language issues:
  - having established our commitment . . .
  - . . . conduct a language audit, and
  - why? how? with what results? (positive or negative).

Thus, the language audit finds a perfect partner in TQM and they, in turn, beget the integrated language strategy:

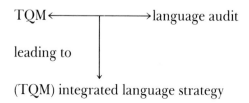

As we saw in chapter 2 ('The Language Audit'), it is vital that commitment exists before, during and after the audit. For Carruthers & Co., the source of this genuine, long-term commitment was TQM.

PRACTICAL EXAMPLES

Quality also has a small 'q'

It may sound simplistic to say that to some people the word 'Quality' simply implies a procedure, a process or an accreditation – or even a training course which they have attended. Nevertheless, there may be an element of truth in this.

The art of Quality or TQM is for these processes and procedures to be translated to *actions* and *attitudes* which become permanent, ingrained and a way of life. At this stage, the word quality can assume its rightful place as an adjective. It then becomes more a matter of the *people* who provide the quality service (providers) and the *people* who understand its worth (industry and commerce) and the *people* who are its ultimate beneficiaries – customers.

TQM also provides us with one very important pointer: we have already learned from other chapters that the quality of providers of language services varies tremendously – from the excellent and truly professional, to services which can be very, very poor. If TQM – or any other vehicle – is to lead to successful language strategies and long-term benefits then the equation has to be completed by top quality provision from the languages industry. It is a quality contract which both parties need to sign. It is a quality process which involves both parties in changes of perception.

A medium-sized company I know of became increasingly involved in Germany and in the German market via a process of acquisitions. An edict from the MD that senior staff in all of the UK locations should learn German was responded to with urgency but with minimal planning. Some approached the local colleges or techs, others private language schools, some approached private tutors, others Yellow Pages.

Within nine months, only one of the courses of tuition was still continuing.

- There had been no planning.
- There had been no Language Audit.
- There had been no coordination.
- There had been no monitoring.

Yet – in total – a lot of time and money had been invested.

The most interesting feature was that the only provider who made a serious attempt to address the issues in terms of a strategy was the provider whose course of tuition continued.

Ultimately, even this approach was rejected. As an outsider to this situation but as somebody who attempts to stand on the 'bridge', I felt very sad that great opportunities had been missed both by the providers and by the organisation.

The firm had experienced growth by acquisition in the German market but the training issue started with a bang and went out with a whimper. What happened? What went wrong? Basically, only one of the providers offered a quality approach. In addition, the organisation itself was unable to link this suggestion of a strategy by one of the providers to its own quality requirements. Nevertheless, the organisation spent a lot of time and money (management training time is expensive), but got it wrong. Nobody derived any benefit. It is doubtful whether the organisation will have a go at language training again, at least for the foreseeable future. Meanwhile, most of the providers involved will probably be puzzled. Above all, who knows to what extent the German side of the operation is suffering?

How could things have evolved differently? Well, in diagrammatic form:

Growth by acquisition in Germany

Commitment via TQM to define the issues

↓

Commitment translated to Language Audit of Needs

↓

Definition by expert or consultant,
in cooperation with the organisation of:
* range of training needs and objectives;
* key personnel;
* coordinated strategy;
* progress evaluation criteria; and
* other language needs (translations, publicity, business culture training)

↓

Competent ← TQM → Long-term benefit to
providers   organisation
working to agreed   (conforming to
specifications   requirements)
(conforming to
requirements).

Poor quality costs

Let us now visit a few examples of the adverse payback of poor quality in terms of language issues.

Publicity or promotional literature

'We cut corners and costs on that item of German publicity literature. The end result was not worthy of our organisation. It reflected badly on us.'

This can be translated thus:

* By what logic were costs pared down and the corners cut? Certainly not by *quality* logic!
* Wasn't the object of the exercise to put the final and permanent gloss on our company?

- What damage has this done to our image, credibility and sales?
- How much had we already invested in the product anyway?
- Whom have we let down? Our customers, our employees, our product, our organisation!

Personnel/HRD policy: the overseas posting

> 'Look, I'm sorry, Richard. I know that you are embarking upon a three-year secondment to France and that you have many obstacles ahead of you with this joint venture. Yes, I know that you only have very rusty O-level French but we just can't release you from your present project for more than a week's crash course – and, in any case, the personnel office in France reckon that once you and your family jump into the water you'll soon be swimming.'

This can be translated thus:

- By what sort of evaluation is one week justified as enough? Not by a *quality* evaluation!
- On what experience is the sink-or-swim analogy being used? (I would like to see some of the people who process overseas postings dropped off in France or Japan for a couple of weeks armed only with a phrasebook!)
- How much is at stake in the joint venture?
- How much vital information and activity will be lost as a result of being linguistically isolated?
- How does the employee feel about the secondment, the new job, his or her family and his employers?

Translation

> 'Look, I really think that £600 for this translation is excessive. Can you get it done any cheaper?'

This can be translated thus:

- What is the translation about? Ah yes, the contract for that job in Spain.
- How much is the contract worth? Well, if we win it – £2 million.
- . . . there's nothing more to say about this particular example other than that there will always be people willing to provide

that one-week crash course without telling you that it's just not enough, or willing to undercut the quote for that translation.

The potential costs of poor quality are horrendous.

Quality distinguishes

Let us now examine the paybacks of paying the real price of getting it right first time. The paybacks are immediate and obvious. They also *distinguish* the organisation because of the image created with outsiders and the good feelings engendered amongst staff.

'That publicity brochure in German went down really well at the Exhibition! It's a really good feeling to know that you are handing out high quality documents.'

'That guy Richard from the UK is settling in really well. He has made a great impression with the French staff, especially on the shopfloor. He makes mistakes but he's already at a level upon which he can build. His wife is settling in well, too. Obviously, Carruthers were able to provide tuition for her too. I'm impressed.'

'That translation of the contract was worth every penny – and more. Do you know, if the translators hadn't pointed out a couple of ambiguities to us we could have been in a real mess. I think they called it "added value". Anyway, we won the contract.'

Customers welcome it

Undoubtedly, the main targets of your TQM-integrated language strategy will be your customers. How reassuring for them when, for example:

- their correspondence is responded to promptly and accurately – even when it is in a foreign language;
- your literature and publicity reads and looks as though it was written in their country and especially for them – which, of course, it should; and

- your staff can converse with them and pay them the ultimate accolade of having made the effort to learn about their language and culture and answer their queries. Wasn't your after-sales engineer telling you only last week how he would never have believed what a difference it would make?

Staff love it

Any organisation's most prized asset is its people.

Individuals are very interested in their personal development and are encouraged when the organisation shows a keen interest in it. As a prime example, we can consider two vastly differing approaches to language training.

The quick-fix approach

- 'Well, we'd better get hold of some tapes for them.'
- 'I suppose that we could provide a lunchtime French conversation class.'
- 'Can the local tech do anything for us?'
- 'I've always managed to get by myself – I don't really know what all the fuss is about.'

The TQM-integrated strategy approach

- 'Who needs to learn and why?'
- 'We'll conduct a language audit.'
- 'We need a policy document on language training. It will be much better if we define the criteria for permission to attend.'
- 'The courses must have attainable objectives and . . .'
- '. . . if we arrange for independent examinations we can enter qualifications on individuals' personnel records.'
- 'We should also consider long-term career plans and the gradual acquisition of language skills . . .'
- '. . . and we should ensure that the right people receive the appropriate intensity of training.'

In the latter scenario, all concerned (including the training providers, the HRD/personnel department, the individual students) can identify with a genuine long-term commitment to the process.

Competitors are doing it!

As we learned earlier in the book, many of our major competitors are already actively pursuing integrated language strategies. Many have been doing so for years.

Why?

'Because English is the world language?'
False. Much of their language training, for example, is in languages other than English. If a German company's target markets happen to include Russia or Japan, then their language training, business culture training and translation services will cover these languages. There are many markets in the world where English alone does not suffice; let's take South America, Eastern Europe and the Pacific Rim just for starters.

'Because they're better than us at languages?'
False. There is no evidence of this other than that in certain countries there is much greater exposure to foreign language studies within the education system and much greater exposure to the English language via the media. There is no visible evidence that would make, for example, a German person a better learner of French than an English person. There *is* an abundance of evidence that if France is one of the key markets of a German company then language training will be a key issue.

Why, then?

Well, TQM may well come into the equation – along with several other issues such as the education system, the expectations of employers and the aspirations of individuals. But what's the *real* difference between the Anglo-American approach and that of Continental Europe and Japan?

One clear difference is that language strategies in many overseas companies are long term as are their overall attitudes to penetrating overseas markets. This is a revealing point because long-termism in one area goes hand in hand with long-termism in the other. These companies have decided that their policies and target markets are long term and, by consequence, so are their attitudes to surrounding issues such as a language strategy.

They have reached the stage at which the word quality assumes a small 'q'. There is simply no debate on *whether* the translation is carried out, or *whether* language training is to be provided. It is simply a question of *how well* it can be done.

It could be that unless more British organisations build long-term and TQM perceptions into their thoughts on language strategies they will be stuck in the 'stop–go' mode which remains fairly prevalent.

Quality is profitable

There is no doubt about this!

I believe that any form of integrated language strategy is also tremendously profitable. It has to be the one which suits you and your organisation and it has to evolve as a long-term strategy.

ENDPIECE

Sitting in her ivory tower, a hostage to those of the academic world who wish to keep her at a mystical distance from the outside world sits Rapunzel, the beautiful embodiment of foreign tongues. As she endlessly brushes her long, long hair and all of the practical knowledge which it holds she wonders whether, if she were to let her hair down, she could ever escape into that big world outside.

But wait! Who approaches! It is a knight of the TQM quality circle on his white charger. She lets down her hair and he climbs the ivory tower and so releases Rapunzel to that world outside. The chimneys and factories are not as ugly as she had been led to believe and Lo! the people are smitten with her beauty and potential.

Throughout my career, I have been invited to and have been happy to address all manner of audiences on the concepts of 'languages for industry and commerce'. Until fairly recently, these audiences were predominantly made up of fellow linguists (translators, students, teachers, trainers and language service providers). I will always totally support the need for professional cooperation, the sharing of experience and the pooling of knowledge. However, I have to say that amidst the spate of 'languages for business' conferences and seminars which '1992 and all that' gave rise to during the late 1980s and early 1990s I was increasingly struck by the almost total absence of representatives of 'business' in the audiences of these particular events.

At times it was rather like being at a party to which the guest of honour had not turned up. The occasional industrialist at such consciousness-raising events was a rare species.

I began to consider how the invitation seemed to them. For one reason or another it clearly was not working!

My reference to Rapunzel is not intended as a slur. It is, I hope, more of a spur. I came to the conclusion that there was more than a bit of the Rapunzel analogy in the *perceptions* of those who had been invited. In some areas, for example language training, the dilemma is even more than one of perception since we have come to live in a political culture which throws together the worlds of education and industry without enabling the parties to tie the knot of real partnership. The result can sometimes be an arranged marriage to which neither party is particularly inclined.

I certainly do not wish to denigrate the good which has resulted from some – but by no means all – of these initiatives. Indeed, there are good and bad providers in both the private and public sectors. However, I must confess to more than lingering doubts about the longer-term benefits of all and sundry having jumped onto the '1992' bandwagon. Now that the bandwagon has run its course, we must all of us – providers and the world of business – tackle the real and *practical* issues of languages and international business.

One way forward is to achieve a radical shift in the perceptions of both partners. In chapter 1 I referred to the need to demystify the perception of languages as an academic, ivory tower. Much more recently, I have found myself rising to the undeniable challenge of addressing and conversing with (the question and answer sessions are always the most important bit!) strictly 'business' audiences at events which are not totally about languages and 1992. I have found that there is still a huge need for a bridge between the professional services provided by many parts of the languages industry and the ultimate beneficiaries of these services – industry and commerce.

Indeed, I would go so far as to predict that the role of 'languages consultant' will quickly emerge as an accepted and much-valued function. Organisations will need to define not only long-term overall strategies but also strategies for particular projects or issues. The languages consultant will be a bridge between the organisation and the welter of private and public sector providers clamouring for business. The winners will undoubtedly be those providers and those users who address the long-term issues of quality. Without such a framework, training courses tend to wither and perish and other language services are conducted on a piecemeal basis. Above all, this enables 'non-quality' providers to survive, and perpetuates the myth – indeed, in strict business terms, the nonsense – of 'language issues' failing to reach their true potential.

Total Quality Management may not ride a white charger but it at least provides an appropriate common language and a realistic set of values for the construction of such a bridge. The alternative is that both sectors will continue to be denied the benefits both of providing and of receiving an excellent service. This would not just be a pity. It would be a denial of the huge and positive potential of the quality language strategies already implemented by our major competitors.

This book contains expert advice on all of the major components of such a strategy. It has enabled Rapunzel to let down her hair and move out into the world of industry and commerce. With flexibility and goodwill from the professional providers of first class language services and the users of these services – coupled with a shared commitment to TQM – the perfect marriage can certainly be made.